IDENTITIES AND ASSERTIONS

IDENTITIES
AND ASSERTIONS

Dalit Women's Narratives

K. Suneetha Rani

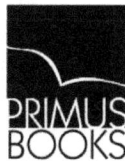

PRIMUS
BOOKS

PRIMUS BOOKS

An imprint of Ratna Sagar P. Ltd.
Virat Bhavan
Mukherjee Nagar Commercial Complex
Delhi 110 009

Offices at

CHENNAI   LUCKNOW

AGRA   AHMEDABAD   BANGALORE   COIMBATORE
DEHRADUN   GUWAHATI   HYDERABAD   JAIPUR   JALANDHAR
KANPUR   KOCHI   KOLKATA   MADURAI   MUMBAI
PATNA   RANCHI   VARANASI

First published 2017

ISBN: 978-93-86552-33-4 (hardback)
ISBN: 978-93-86552-34-1 (POD)

PUBLISHED BY PRIMUS BOOKS

Laser typeset by Guru Typograph Technology
Crossings Republic, Ghaziabad 201009
Printed and bound in India by Replika Press Pvt. Ltd.

Contents

Preface

THIS BOOK IS based on the fieldwork that I conducted between 2003 and 2005. However, I have discussed the issues such as the identity discourse and Dalit Feminism to build a discourse around the oral narratives with the help of published literature and literary movements closely working together with caste and regional movements.

First, I must thank the Dalit women whose experiences have become the texts for this project. But for their cooperation and time, this project would not have materialized. Many people contributed to my project at various stages by giving valuable suggestions, helping with fieldwork, extending their writings, making corrections and in various other capacities. I profusely thank each and every one of them for their patience, enthusiasm and interest. Apart from many other friends, colleagues and students who helped me with the documentation and analysis, I specially thank Sahitya Akademi for awarding me Junior Fellowship to work on this project and Professor Ghanta Chakrapani for his inputs, Professor V. Krishna, Dr M.M. Vinodini and Mr Lingaraju for helping me with fieldwork.

1

Introduction

OVEMENT AND LITERATURE, written as well as oral,
published and unpublished are interconnected in their
purpose and impact in most situations of conflict,
struggle and protest. We see a similar situation in the Telugu
speaking states from late nineteenth century, in the Dalit context.
Dalit literature marked and was also influenced by the happenings
in that century. In that sense it functioned as an alternative history
and counter memory as well. We cannot separate movement and
literature in this context, also because most of the Dalit writers
turned out to be activists in the Dalit movement.

This chapter attempts to draw an outline of the Dalit
movement and Dalit literature in the Telugu speaking region.
It is in no way a comprehensive history of Dalit movement
and Dalit literature. It is an attempt to map the historical
developments and understand the context in which the Dalit
women's narratives were recorded and analysed. It is an attempt
to recapitulate the history of Dalit movement and literature that
has already been documented and discussed by several other

scholars whose work will be extensively referred to in this chapter. Although the main argument of this book concentrates on women's narratives, this chapter does not focus on women but only traces how women were participating actively at various stages of the movement and the literature.

Late nineteenth century in India witnessed the emergence of activists such as Jyotirao Phule, Savitribai Phule, Tarabai Shinde and others from the depressed classes who strived for the betterment of women and the disadvantaged sections. They contributed to a major leap in the history of the marginalized communities by working towards educating them. Their efforts disseminated the ideas of progress, opened avenues for the lower castes towards social and economic mobility and introduced a breakthrough in the education system established by the British. While they were fighting against the colonial rule, they were also discussing how the colonizer's language and education could help the downtrodden from the internal colonization that they were subjected to for ages.

In twentieth century, as Gail Omvedt rightly puts it, '... while Gandhi represented in cultural terms a reformist Hinduism, rising non-Brahmin movements in western and southern India and scattered Dalit movements throughout the country put forward a challenge to Hinduism itself with new, low caste, peasant and regional community identities'.[1] Multiple influences and developments contributed to the emergence of Dalit consciousness. Again, to quote Omvedt,

Worker and peasant struggles, Gandhism, Hindu–Muslim tensions and the rise of Hindu nationalism, and non-Brahmin political formations (the Justice party in south India, the Non-Brahmin party in Bombay) all provided the ideological and organizational environment within which early Dalit organizing took place. At the same time, Dalit initiatives put pressures on these sections, making the issue of 'untouchability' a politically salient one.[2]

Two choices and two paths were open for Dalits that could lead them in different directions. They had the choice to go back to the fold of Hinduism by following Gandhi's call for the Ram Raj or they could go in the direction of their autonomy with the help of movements such as the Communist movement. This 'two-choice'–'two-path' option that Omvedt refers to could be extended to the option of ideologies that they had between M.K. Gandhi and B.R. Ambedkar. While one talked about reforming of the society and the reforming of Harijans, the other gave a call for dismantling of the caste system to lay the foundations for an egalitarian society which was the only means of liberation for Dalits. While one tried to reiterate an enduring untouchable, the other moulded a fighting activist. The initial phase witnessed Dalit leanings towards Gandhian thought and reform.

Dalit communities in the Telugu speaking land were also greatly influenced by Gandhi. Some non-Dalit leaders influenced by the Gandhian ideology voiced the need for upliftment of lower castes and eradication of untouchability. During 1906–39, Dalit leaders rebelled against three aspects, i.e. 'The economic deprivation resulting from their status, denial of access to social and civic communities by Brahmins and persecutions based on caste inferiority'.[3] The major contribution came from the Dalit communities when they started stepping into the political spaces.

Dalit activities in Hyderabad began to gain momentum even before the radical 1930s. A new generation of educated and radical Dalits rejected the panchama[4] and the Harijan identities and organized themselves as Adi Andhras. Madari Bhagya Reddy Varma organized Andhra Desa First Panchama Conference in Bezawada from 4 to 6 November in 1917. 'They employed popular means like conducting Harikatha Kalakshepams, Bhajan Mandalis on one hand and establishment of newspapers/journals on the other' (Chinna Rao 101).

3

D.R. Nagaraj makes very important observations about this period. It is during this reformist period influenced by Gandhi that we come across the call for the purification of the upper castes to eradicate untouchability and accept 'untouchables' which resulted in a call for the self-purification of Dalits as a ritual in Harijan movement. It is true that some Dalit writers and activists of the period were influenced by Gandhian thought and were working towards the elimination of untouchability but they were also propagating the reformation of the Harijans. Nagaraj continues his argument about this crucial phase in Dalit movement by saying that this self-purification of upper castes projected them as great people in front of whom the Dalits were made to feel belittled. As he rightly points out, Dalit literature and movement of this period were located between the social rage and the spiritual quest and combined despair and hope. Nagaraj's concept of 'wilful amnesia' brilliantly sums up this particular phase of Dalit literature and movement when Dalits were made to embrace amnesia about the treatment meted out to them for generations and fit into the reform mode.[5]

Women like Arigey Lalitadevi, Rajamanidevi, Katta Ramakka and Eswaribai played very active role in the Adi Hindu movement along with M.L. Adaiah, J.H. Subbaiah, Vemula Kurmaiah, Kusuma Dharmanna and Kusuma Venkatramaiah, Bhagya Reddy Varma, Arigey Ramaswamy and S. Venkatrao. This movement worked to achieve unity between the depressed and untouchable castes to fight against the social evils such as *jogini* system,[6] animal sacrifice and child marriage and also towards education for the marginalized in the twin cities of Hyderabad and Secunderabad. M.L. Adaiah established an organization to give free education to children who were barred from joining the schools due to their caste identity. The Adi Hindu leaders Rangamma, Katta Ramakka and Bhagya Reddy Varma established Adi Hindu Girls School in Isamia Bazar,

Hyderabad in 1920. Katta Ramakka established Payal School in Gasmandi for Mala and Madiga children and another school in Kalvabasti for the orphaned, street children. Adi Hindu Social Service League was established and a magazine *Bhagyanagar* was printed in the press run by the leaders of the movement. They were neither with the Nizam rule nor with the freedom struggle led by the *savarna* (caste Hindus; castes within the fold of Hinduism) Hindu leaders of the Hindu Mahasabha. They followed alternative strategies to simultaneously fight against the caste system as well as the state control.[7] While the coastal districts also witnessed many Dalit activists who established schools for Dalit children, Christianity played a major role in educating Dalit children in this region.

The employees organized themselves as SC Employees Association and others during 1930s and 40s. Kancha Ilaiah acknowledges the influence of the communist movement on Dalits during this time. They could understand the movement and associate themselves with it as working class people. As he rightly points out, during this period, Dr B.R. Ambedkar and his thought impacted the Dalit movement to choose an altogether different perspective from the Gandhian and Communist ideologies. He became an icon of inspiration for Dalits.[8] In 1936, Dr B.R. Ambedkar started Akhila Bharatha Scheduled Kulala Samakhya and Bhagya Reddy Varma, Venkat Rao and Arigey Ramaswamy actively carried it forward in Hyderabad and Secunderabad. It majorly fought for the unity of Dalits working for the social and political rights of Dalits and against the inequalities between Dalit castes. This phase was called the time of psychological revolution. Many Dalit women such as Arigey Lalitadevi, Rajamanidevi, Eswaribai, Katta Ramakka and others worked in this movement for Dalit women's rights.[9]

An extension of Dalit women's participation in the movement and politics can be seen in teaching. Dalit teachers such as Jala

Mangamma and Tadi Nagamma faced serious resentment from students and parents. Upper caste parents refused to send their children to study under Dalit teachers. Sometimes the Dalit teachers taught a couple of students who attended the school and some other times they sat through the day alone in the school with no students around.[10] This phase can be called the most significant in terms of consolidation of Dalit women's participation in various fields of protest movements. Not only did they step into political spaces but they also occupied political positions. The contribution of one such Dalit woman politician, S. Sadalakshmi is discussed in detail in later chapters.

A complete turn in the Dalit movement came with the ghastly incidents of violence on Dalits in the village of Karamchedu in July 1985. In Kancha Ilaiah's words, 'Karamchedu is a point of departure both for Andhra political history and for the Ambedkarite movement because Andhra politics began to undergo a metamorphosis in terms of its very political discourse'.[11] A Madiga woman objected to a Kamma boy using drinking water for washing his buffaloes. The enraged upper castes ruthlessly murdered six Dalits. As has been discussed earlier in this chapter, there had been efforts and movements towards mobilizing Dalits before the Karamchedu incident. However, it was this incident that organized Dalits into an independent movement, united them and clearly defined violent casteist discrimination by fighting against it through activism and literature.

The legal struggle continued for more than a decade. Meantime some from the victims' community and offenders' community were dead and some offenders escaped with little or no punishment. Another major incident that angered Dalits and united them once again was the Chundur carnage in August 1991 where eight Dalits were murdered by a Reddy landlord. There are several other such incidents that repeatedly challenged the status of Dalits in society and attempted to continue to condemn them to untouchability and exploitation. However, Dalits have been fighting untiringly to eliminate all forms of discrimination. The later movements as those mentioned above gave rise to Dalit leaders like Katti Padma Rao, Bojja Tarakam, Boyi Bheemanna and others. As Kancha Ilaiah observes,

The post Karamchedu period in fact produced several Dalit leaders, speakers, writers and songsters who became the pillars of Dalitbahujan consciousness. This consciousness began to construct a theory of its own liberation. Political autonomy of Dalitbahujan organic intellectuals began to emerge in this atmosphere, which finally led to the formation of Dalit Maha Sabha, Bahujan Republic Party and Bahujan Samaj Party by K.G. Satyamurthy, a former communist revolutionary.[12]

Dalit women stood in the forefront of these movements to protest against the upper caste atrocities on Dalits. Women like Suvartamma, Yesamma, Alisamma, Gracamma, Leela Kumari, Lakshmi Theresa and others played an instrumental role in these movements. Gogu Shyamala, in her introduction to *Nallapoddu* emphatically states that Dalit women were the foundations of the organizations that formed in 1983. To quote from Kancha Ilaiah, again,

The Karamchedu camp also focused the militancy of Dalit women very sharply. Dalit women stood in the forefront of the struggle. Of course, at one level the male leadership used the women's militancy as a check against the state repression but at another level it did not put any special effort to push any visible woman leader from among the ranks of Dalit women. Also, the ground reality was such that there were hardly any educated women who could push themselves to the status of leading cadre. The women's militancy, therefore, expressed itself as mass collective militancy. However, it must be pointed out that with regard to man-woman relationship, the Dalit movement drew heavily from the patriarchal society on the one hand and the patriarchal communist and bourgeois parties on the other. Though

Phule, Periyar and Ambedkar gave more emphasis to women's equality than their contemporary communist and bourgeois leaders, it has not yet acquired an organizational legitimacy. The discourse on man–woman equality has not become a key discourse even in the Dalit movement.[13]

This point about women's status in Dalit movements and the gender dynamics within Dalit communities frequently comes up for discussion in Dalit women's writing.

These movements were people's movements where people, along with the leaders fought serious battles. In the words of Challapalli Swarooparani,

An ideological change emerged in Dalit movement in the decade of 2000. The slogan of Dalit self-esteem that echoed during Karamchedu movement, Dalit literature in response to that and the Madiga Dandora movement that surged up in the second half of 1990s brought in a great movement among the Dalit Bahujan communities. The Madiga Dandora movement that started with a demand for categorizing the S.C. reservations based on the population kindled identity consciousness among Dalit subcastes, tribals and hundreds of backward castes. It gave the self-esteem to proudly declare that 'I belong' to a certain caste for many castes and tribes that hesitated to name their caste all these years. While the Dalit Bahujans broadly united under the umbrella of Dalit during Karamchedu and Chunduru Dalit movement, it moved towards specificity with the Dandora movement. It can be said that every oppressed caste started to question about its status in the society with the identity consciousness.[14]

Another crucial turn came in the region with the continual upsurge of Telangana movement. Telangana fought simultaneously against the Nizam rule and the British rule before the Indian independence. It fought for its independent status as the state of Telangana for more than six decades. It raised issues related to education, development, language, religion, economic mobility and regional differences. It is interesting to see how Dalit writers started to declare their multifaceted but pointed identities based on their caste, class, region and gender. This declaration of identity declared their loyalty to the related movements as well.

While Gogu Shyamala classifies various phases of Dalit movement and literature from a woman's perspective in her introduction to her book *Nallapoddu*, Challapalli Swarooparani seems to identify two major phases of the twentieth-century Dalit movement and literature with the Karamchedu incident as the central point. She says,

Karamchedu is a milestone in the history of Dalit movement and the Dalit literary and cultural history. The Dalit movement that started in protest against the massacre of the Madigawada by the upper caste feudal lords in Karamchedu village of Prakasam district in 1985 gave rise to a new protest literature. After Karamchedu, the Dalit youth whose blood was boiling about the massacre of Dalits by upper castes in Chunduru, Neerukonda, Podirikuppam, Vempenta and other places gave the form of poetry to their anger.[15]

She continues to say that, 'Dalit literature prior to Karamchedu expressed the Dalit consciousness and its reformist nature of those times. Initial writers wrote as if they were requesting the upper caste people to recognize them as human beings while a Dalit protest voice can be heard in the literature after Karamchedu.'[16]

In the twentieth century, writers such as Gurram Jashua, Jala Rangaswamy, Kusuma Dharmanna, Boyi Bheemanna and others tremendously contributed to Dalit literature with their diverse voices and forms of writing. However, all of them were writing also to the upper castes to make them understand the patterns of exploitation and discrimination that they inflicted on their fellow beings and to transform themselves into better human beings. This transformative writing certainly marked the element of protest in Dalit literature. The forms adopted, the tone employed and the solutions suggested were more of negotiation

9

in nature than of rebellion though the writers raised very serious issues that shook the foundations of the casteist society.

The later phase of Dalit literature, post-Karamchedu, to borrow the term from Challapalli Swarooparani and Kancha Ilaiah, was more questioning and rebelling in its content and tone. Large number of Dalit writers started to publish in journals, anthologies and independent books. The first major anthology of Dalit writing in Telugu was *Chikkanavutunna Paata*[17] edited by G. Lakshminarasaiah and Tripuraneni Srinivas. This anthology did not include any Dalit woman writer while the later anthologies of Dalit writing such as *Gundedappu*[18] and *Padunekkina Paata*[19] included some women writers. *Gunde Dappu* had two poems by Challapalli Swarooparani and *Padunekkina Paata*, which was brought out as a continuation of *Chikkanavutunna Paata* had poems by Dalit and Bahujan women. Dalit writers like Kolakaluri Enoch, P. Sivasagar, Katti Padmarao, Satish Chander, Yendluri Sudhakar, Shikhamani, Nagappagari Sundarraju, Madduri Nageshbabu, Kalekuri Prasad, Paidi Tereshbabu, Gundedappu Kanakaih, Darla Venkateswarrao, Kalyana Rao, Chilukuri Devaputra, Vemula Ellaih and others published phenomenal writings.[20] These writers wrote on different aspects of Dalit life and in different genres, some from a Dalit perspective, some others from a Marxist perspective. But, all of them questioned the hierarchical caste system and the deep-rooted brahmanical ideology.

Similarly, Dalit women writers also experimented with different genres and touched upon different aspects of Dalit women's life. *Nallapoddu*, the first comprehensive collection of Dalit women's writing in Telugu edited by Gogu Shyamala cites Philip B. Nagaratnamma (1890–1960) as the first Dalit woman writer, who wrote and translated songs into Telugu. Vesapogu Gulbanamma (1905–71) wrote songs in praise of Christianity. Early writers like Tadi Nagamma and Jala Mangamma were teachers and activists who played an active role in different movements. Not all early Dalit women writers revealed their social identities but wrote under the larger agenda of religion, nation, freedom struggle, education for women, class differences, poverty and exploitation. We can clearly see the writers' purpose to locate themselves as the Telugu women writers without associating and affiliating themselves with any caste identities or caste movements. While Namburi Paripurna of this period wrote with Marxist and gender consciousness, Kolakaluri Swarooparani wrote with a clear Dalit perspective. Another woman writer who is continuing to write is B. Vijayabharathi, who has successfully used the genre of prose to expose the casteist and patriarchal notions and relationships in the Hindu classics. However, it is the post-Karamchedu Dalit movement that brought in a radical change in the expression of Dalit writers. Dalit Panther movement emerging in Maharashtra on the model of Black Panther movement had a great impact on Dalit movement in the Telugu-speaking region. Karamchedu and Chunduru incidents also equally kindled the fire of protest in the Dalit movement.

Women writers of this period include Varre Rani, Challapalli Swarooparani, Jajula Gowri, M.M. Vinodini, Joopaka Subhadra, Gogu Shyamala, Jhansi K.V. Kumari, Putla Hemalatha, Jalli Indira, Surepalli Sujatha and others. They published poetry, short fiction, novels, prose and drama. They edited collections of poetry, short fiction and prose. They also documented biographies and personal narratives. The subcaste, religious, regional and generational identities that inform their writings will be discussed in detail in the chapter on the identity discourse.

This book focuses on the construction of self through narratives. It would be relevant to examine the Dalit autobiographies published in Telugu before we analyse the collected personal narratives of Dalit women. It is an accepted fact that most of Dalit literature is autobiographical in nature. However, choice of the genre and place/space of publication is also very important in discussing the writer's intention, expectation and the outcome. Self-profiling is one of the milestones in the politics of the marginalized as it intends to construct the self and deconstruct the other.

The very first Dalit autobiography in Telugu is *Naa Katha*[21] by Gurram Jashuva. His long poem *Gabbilam*[22] also echoes autobiographical characteristics. It traces the journey of a bat from darkness outside into the darkness in the sanctum sanctorum. He compares himself as a Dalit to a bat as a banned creature and wonders how the bat has an entry into the temple while he does not have. He requests the bat to convey his predicament to the god as the bat rests very close to the god in the dark corners of the temple. Later Nagappagari Sundarraju and Yendluri Sudhakar published collections of short fiction, *Madigodu*[23] and *Mallemoggala Godugu*[24] respectively which are autobiographical in nature. Kalyana Rao's novel *Antaraani Vasantam*[25] documents the family history and from there the community history by erasing the autobiographical self and yet calling the novel autobiographical. *Khakibatukulu*[26] by Spartacus also documented the institution of police in pre- and post-independent India from a lower caste and class perspective.

Nallapoddu edited by Gogu Shyamala was the first comprehensive collection of Dalit women's writing in Telugu. Published in 2003, it contains introduction to 54 Dalit women writers and their writings. Each introduction could be taken as a personal narrative and each writing as autobiographical since the self of the writer appears somewhere or the other in their writings. Gogu Shyamala went on to publish collections of short stories, life story of Sadalakshmi and several articles. She also edited *Nallaregadi Sallu*,[27] a collection of Madiga subcaste women's short fiction, along with Joopaka Subhadra. Subhadra is known not only for her short stories and poetry but also for her prose writings such as her columns. She has published collections of short fiction and poetry. Her column *Maakka Mukkupulla Geenne Poyindi* in *Bhumika Strivada Patrika* has been unveiling crucial discussions about caste, class, gender, religion and region.

Jajula Gowri is another significant Dalit woman writer from Telangana. Married at a very early age, Gowri continued her education and got a Ph.D. in Law. She has written some poetry, a collection of short stories *Mannubuvva*[28] and a novel *Voyinam*.[29] Although most of her short stories run in first person narrative, there are some specific stories where it is her life and her childhood self that speak out. Like any other marginalized writers, Dalit women are also concentrating more and more on the self-writing without any inhibitions and fears.

The other two prominent Dalit women writers are Challa-palli Swarooparani and M.M. Vinodini from the Andhra region. Swarooparani's collection of poetry *Mankenapoovu*[30] locates her amidst Dalit communities but also relocates her in the midst of the educated, violent men in Dalit communities as well as outside. She writes the life stories of her people such as her mother, grandmother and grandfather. She brilliantly captures the voices of the *jogini* women who are branded as promiscuous even before they are born. Swarooparani has also attempted short fiction and critical literary essays. Most of her work echoes her autobiographical self, either in terms of her experience or in terms of her ideology.

Similarly, M.M. Vinodini writes from a Dalit Christian woman's perspective. Most of her own experiences have gone on to become her poetry, short fiction and prose writing. Her poetry traces the Dalit Christian dilemma and insecurity in the midst of the Hinduized casteist society and state. Her stories also record the manifestation of casteist attitudes in various patterns and in varied fields and how Dalits especially Dalit women counter them in their own way. Her articles on pedagogy have raised crucial questions about teaching of Telugu literature. She argues how the casteist and patriarchal Telugu literature courses and the texts taught prove humiliating for women and marginalized sections and how they function as instruction material for the discriminating sections. This autobiographical self of a teacher succeeds in documenting the need for a change in the education system and her personal experience as a student, researcher, teacher and supervisor becomes the basis for this.

Several other Dalit autobiographical narratives in various genres have been published. But, like any other working class and marginalized communities, Dalits also have a very strong tradition of oral literature and theatre. For generations they have been singing the folk forms, story songs, oggukatha, burrakatha, veedhi bhagavatham and others. Their cultural performances such as Jambapuranam, Chenna Puranam, Yellamma Katha, Allirani Katha, Chindu Bhagavatham and others have been rich sources of their knowledge and heritage. Some attempts were made to document these art forms but most of the oral tradition still remains unrecorded. However, there was some attempt to document the life stories of the Dalit artists. The story of Chindu Yellamma, a rebellious Chindu woman who made her name in the history of Dalit folk arts, has been recorded and published as *Nenu Chindula Yellammanu*.[31] Similarly, the story of Chandrasri, a Dalit woman singer and performer who established a Dalit Women's Theatre has been documented post-humously through the narratives of the people who interacted with her.[32]

It is against this backdrop that I am going to analyse the Dalit women's narratives in this book informed by the various debates around the identity questions of Dalit women as articulated and debated by Dalit movement and Dalit literature. It is in this context that I choose to use Dalit women's writing in Telugu as the framework to analyse the Dalit women's oral narratives. Despite the differences between writing women and working women, the multidimensional Dalit women's consciousness brings them together in their journey towards assertion of their identity.

NOTES

1. *Dalits and the Democratic Revolution: Dr Ambedkar and the Dalit Movement in Colonial India*, New Delhi: Sage Publications, 1994, p. 106.
2. Ibid., pp. 106–7.
3. Yagati Chinna Rao, *Writing Dalit History and Other Essays*, New Delhi: Kanishka Publishers and Distributors, 2007, p. 81.
4. Outside the four varnas, the fifth varna, 'untouchable' communities.
5. D.R. Nagaraj, *The Flaming Feet and Other Essays: The Dalit Movement in India*, Prithvi Datta and Chandra Shobhi, eds., Ranikhet: Permanent Black, 2010.
6. Dalit devadasi system in which a Dalit girl is devoted to the temple in the village and is thereby forced into sex work.
7. Gogu Shyamala, ed., *Nallapoddu: Dalita Streela Sahityam 1921–2002*, Hyderabad: Hyderabad Book Trust, 2003, p. 7.
8. Kancha Ilaiah, 'Caste or Class or Caste-Class: A Study in Dalitbahujan Consciousness and Struggles in Andhra Pradesh in 1980s', in *Class, Caste, Gender*, ed. Manoranjan Mohanty, New Delhi: Sage Publications, 2004, pp. 227–55.
9. Ibid., pp. 9–10.
10. Ibid., p. 32.
11. Ibid., p. 230.
12. Ibid., p. 231.
13. Ibid., pp. 241–2.
14. Challapalli Swarooparani, *Asthitva Gaanam: A Collection of Essays*, Vijayawada: Mythri Prachuranalu, 2012, pp. 67–8.
15. Ibid., p. 58.
16. Ibid., p. 59.
17. G. Lakshminarasaiah and Tripuraneni Srinivas, eds., *Chikkanavutunna Paata: Dalita Kavitvamu*, Hyderabad: Kavitvam Prachuranalu, 1995.
18. Patteti Rajasekhar and Nagappagari Sundarraju, eds., *Gundedappu: Dalita Kavita Sankalanam*, Hyderabad: Dalita Sahitya Vedika, 1995.
19. G. Lakshminarasaiah, ed., *Padunekkina Paata: Dalita Kavitvam*, Vijayawada: Dalita Sana Prachuranalu, 1996.
20. I have briefly referred to the subcaste debate earlier. It will be taken up in detail with reference to Dalit women writers in the chapter on the identity discourse. I have not mentioned the subcaste identities of these writers as I am using the word 'Dalit' as a political

category but not as a caste category. This is how Dalit activists have defined the term and how it is being used in the context of political movements.

21. Gurram Jashuva, *Naa Katha: My Story,* Vijayawada: Hemalatha Lavanam, 1996 (1966).

22. Gurram Jashuva, *Gabbilam: Bat,* Hyderabad:Visalanadhra Publishing House, 2007 (1941).

23. Nagappagari Sundarraju, *Madigodu: Nagappagari Sundarraju Kathalu,* Hyderabad: Madiga Sahitya Vedika, 1997.

24. Yendluri Sudhakar, *Mallemoggala Godugu: Madiga Kathalu,* Hyderabad: Dandora Prachuranalu, 1999.

25. G. Kalyana Rao, *Antaraani Vasantam,* Hyderabad:Viplava Rachayitala Sangham, 2000.

26. G. Mohanarao (Spartacus), *Khakibatukulu,* Tenali: Pratyusha Publications, 1998.

27. Gogu Shyamala and Joopaka Subhadra, eds., *Nallaregadi Sallu: Madiga Upakulala Adolla Kathalu,* Hyderabad: Mysavva Publications, 2006.

28. Jajula Gowri, *Mannubuvva: Kathalu,* Hyderabad: Samajika Tatvika Viswavidyalayam, 2004.

29. Jajula Gowri, *Voyinam: Telangana Navala,* Hyderabad:Vishala Sahitya Academy, 2012.

30. Challapalli Swarooparani, *Mankenapoovu: Kavitvam,* Hyderabad, 2005.

31. K. Muthyam, ed., comp., *Nenu Chindula Yellammanu: Chindu Bhagavatham Atmakatha,* Hyderabad: Drishti, 2006.

32. Joopaka Subhadra, ed., *Chandrasri Yaadilo: Rachanala Sankalanam,* Hyderabad: Mattipulu Rachayitrula Vedika, 2013.

2

The Identity Discourse

IDENTITY HAS ALWAYS been a crucial issue in Dalit movement. Dalits have been struggling to dismantle the label of 'untouchability' that society has inflicted on them. The clash between the identity that has been 'allotted' to them and the identity that they want to establish gets transformed into agony, anguish, anger, contempt and revolt. Any exploitation or discrimination is based on the identity of a person, be it on the basis of the individual or the community. Hence, identity assumes such importance in any discourse.

Richard Jenkins, a Sociologist, says, 'Identity is often in the eye of the beholder' (Jenkins 2).[1] In the case of Dalit women's writing, this conflict between identities becomes much more pertinent because it is keeping the beholder's concept of the identity in view that Dalit writers write to contradict the mainstream hegemonic notions about Dalit women and voice their demand for restructuring of the casteist and patriarchal society on the principles of equality. It is to say that the beholder has been unjust, biased and callous that Dalit writers write strongly condemning the identity that is thrust on them leading to their predicament as outcastes.

It is true that society and social identity are intertwined and interdependent. Society decides the social identities of people and social identities decide the nature of society. In a highly stratified society like India, social identities function as dividing walls and boundaries. Society, indeed, thrives on this capacity of social identities to divide and rule. As Jenkins says it is the power and politics that are central to the questions of identity because power and politics create social identities to vest power in a few people and marginalize others. Identities play a crucial role in power politics.

However, as has been discussed above, there are always voices that counter such power politics in their own way be it at the individual level or at the community level. This book focuses on the narratives of women who are not actively part of any major or obvious movement in order to understand how as individuals they negotiate with the power structures to resist the hierarchy and assert themselves. These narratives do not demand for a radical alteration of the society nor do they refuse to work in the existing system. Their strategy is to work in the system but work for change that can contribute to betterment of their status in society. Their opinions, experiences, strategies and achievements are diverse and thus add varied dimensions to the Dalit woman's consciousness.

Iris Marion Young's discussion of Toril Moi's concept of lived body experience can be invoked here to understand the complex identities of Dalit women as presented in their narratives. While Toril Moi proposes that the existential phenomenological category of the lived body is a richer and more flexible concept than gender for theorizing the socially constituted experience of women and men than concepts of either sex or gender and that the lived body is particular in its morphology, material similarities and differences from other bodies,[2] Iris Young, agreeing with

Moi, argues that 'this proposal should not mean dispensing with a category of gender, but rather confining its use to analysis of social structures for the purposes of understanding certain specific relations of power, opportunity, and resource distribution'.[3]

The multifaceted identities of narrators in this book based on their gender, caste, religion, location and occupation position them along with others as individuals and as part of communities. But, the changing combinations of these identities and their experiences and their responses as individuals to certain identities lead us towards their lived body experiences. Their identities and experiences do not necessarily need to fall under either celebration or jeopardy of their identity. While they live and experience as individuals, they also connect themselves constantly with the larger identities and collective consciousness which reiterates the fact that identities are relational and dynamic. This clearly comes out in the narratives when the speakers constantly move between 'I' and 'We'.

Anupama Rao, capturing the milestones in the process of 'naming' the 'untouchables', says,

Simply put, Ambedkar provided the set of political idioms that most effectively converted the negative identity of the untouchables into the political potentiality and historical agency of the Dalit. Ambedkar first used the term *dalit* in his journal, *Bahishkrit Bharat* (Outcaste India), in 1928, where he characterized being Dalit as the experience of deprivation, marginalization, and stigmatization. Dalit indexed both subject of suffering and revolutionary agent, and it was posed against 'Harijan'—people of god or 'Hari', first used by M.K. Gandhi in 1933 to describe 'men of God abandoned by society', a term abhorred by many *dalits* for its paternalism. Indeed, the politics of naming is deeply consequential for the politics of recognition. If names are also 'claims to certain identities, properties, or entitlement', it is through the 'reiterative process of naming' that those identities become fixed and meaningful in the first place. The politics of naming thus secures new relationships between words and bodies, between ways of being and ways of seeing and speaking within the social field. 'In this case, the politics of the name also reflects a deeper paradox of Dalit politics that derives from the fact that the term "Dalit" is both analytic and prescriptive: *it defines the historical structures and practices of dispossession that experientially mark someone as Dalit and simultaneously identifies the Dalit as someone seeking to escape those same structures.*'[4]

Naming is one of the political strategies that the dominant sections use to establish and preserve the hegemony. This naming could also manifest as re-naming either in appropriation or in resistance. Self-naming, de-naming or re-naming by Dalits in order to subvert their naming has taken place in different ways in order to reassert their dignity and self-esteem. Whether it is the political term Dalit or the constitutional term scheduled castes or the subcaste identities such as Mala and Madiga, they have always tried to hit back at the oppressive patterns of brahmanical ideology and defined the names and categories according to their terms of protest. Words have acquired new meanings in the terminology of Dalit movements. Gopal Guru concludes his article 'The Language of Dalit-Bahujan Political Discourse' by saying that 'The Dalit category is historically arrived at, sociologically presented and discursively constituted'.[5]

However, it has not always been the question of uniting or giving a common name of the political category of Dalit. It was also about the question of subcastes, religions, regions and specificities. Dalit itself is not a homogeneous category. Definition of the term Dalit itself is being debated. If we confine the category Dalit to 'untouchables' alone, as this project has done, even then there are many categories among Dalits. Basically, this project takes into consideration the narratives in Telugu, the major and the official language of Andhra Pradesh and Telangana. There are 44 scheduled castes in Andhra Pradesh[6] as the word Dalit is defined here. Among these, some twenty castes have hardly any representation in education, employment, legislation and movements. So, it is basically the glaring presence of a few and absence of many scheduled castes that we come across when we examine the Dalit situation in Andhra Pradesh. This absence and presence have always led to a conflict between the dominant and the not dominant sections among Dalits. The demand for a separate share for Madigas in reservations for scheduled castes has been a concern of Madigas for a long time now. N. Sudhakar Rao quotes T.R. Singh[7] in his article 'The Structure of South Indian Untouchable Castes: A View',[8] who observes that Madiga is the central caste in Telangana region with six satellite castes. The subcastes are Sangari (spiritual guides, preachers of caste-defined moral standards, caste rules and conduct), Binedu or Baindla, Erupula (participate in village rituals), Sindu or Chindu (drama troupers who also supply women dedicated to goddess Matangi), Mashin (acrobats) and Dakkalis (beggars).

In this context, identities have assumed sharpness and unique-ness and they have been constantly changing based on the community's role in Movements, its demands and commitments. Assertive declaration of one's caste identity and prefixing or suffixing the caste or subcaste identities to people's names is the best example for this. To cite a specific example, Manda Krishna, the leader of Madiga movement in Andhra, became Manda Krishna Madiga reiterating not only his and his community's identity but also subverting the connotations associated by the society to his caste identity. Dalit identity is no longer an identity to be hidden but a matter of pride to be declared.

Literature has been produced in favour of and against these Movements by Dalits as well as non-Dalits.[9] The Madiga Dandora movement in the Telugu speaking region very soon gained momentum and became a political movement from a subcaste movement. It brought into light the fact about the heterogeneity of the Dalit communities and the replication of the hierarchical caste system in the mainstream society in the Dalit communities as well. As inequality has always been linked to the inequalities in opportunities, entitlements and representations, the Dalit subcastes were not equally represented and developed and they could not articulate their concerns and predicaments. Dandora movement brought all these points to the forefront and argued for their share in the reservations in education and employment according to their ratio in the population. This population ratio and the lack of opportunities become more crucial in the Telangana region as the Madiga population is more than any other subcastes in this region. Some, including the Dalits and the non-Dalits have perceived this movement as a separatist movement that will affect the unity and power of the Dalit movement. However, it has also been observed and argued that development and mobility have been accessed by Dalit communities differently based on their subcaste and region.

Yendluri Sudhakar's long poem *Vargeekaraneeyam* (the saga of categorization)[10] published in 2004 brings in some such issues for discussion. The title and the theme of the poem are about the categorization and the subtitle calls it a long Dalit poem. This 'naming' declares the political choice of being a Dalit as well as the specific identity of the subcaste and the issues built around it. He declares solidarity with other marginalized Dalit subcastes, points out that Madiga women were subjected to bonded labour and sexual exploitation as Dalit devadasis and attributes the progress of the dominant Dalit subcaste to their conversion into Christianity and thereby winning a large share of reservations. He compares this subcaste struggle to the battle between Pandavas and Kauravas in Mahabharatha and hopes that this Mahabharatha does not end in Kurukshetra but in truce.

Such subcaste consciousness is expressed by Dalit subcaste women writers who have not only contributed to the anthologies of Madiga writings but also exclusively edited collections of writings such as *Nallaregatisallu: Madiga Upakulala*

Adolla Kathalu.[11] The collection includes stories by Dalit and non-Dalit, men and women, Telangana and non-Telangana writers. However, these stories are centred around Madiga and other subcaste women. Two different introductions by the two editors raise significant issues about the need to document the stories of Madiga and other subcaste women and also come up with insightful definitions. Joopaka Subhadra reiterates that Dalit woman is a political category and the Madiga subcaste woman is a specific political category and a cultural construct. She explains that Madiga and other subcaste women were mostly relegated from the mainstream as well as Dalit discourse and literatures and that even the first anthology of Dalit women's writing in Telugu *Nallapoddu* also included mostly Mala women from the coastal Andhra. So, this collection fills that glaring gap. Gogu Shyamala in her Introduction describes this book as the book of life of the original inhabitants of this country surging up from the original inhabitant women's experiences of violence, sweat, blood and oppression. Shyamala's introduction declares solidarity with all the artisan working classes while acknowledging the inspiration for this book to the Chindu performer Yellamma.

More important identity in the context of the location of the research that I have chosen—that of Telangana districts—is the regional identity. What is revealed here is not just the assertion of belonging to a region but also a demand for respect for a language, culture, lifestyle as well as for the status of a separate state. When this research was being conducted during 2003–5, Telangana had been the aspiration of people for almost 60 years. But, now it is a destination that has been realized. The language that was used by Dalit writers during this phase is very symbolic to understand how they wanted to establish a unique identity for themselves as Dalits from Telangana, sometimes even specifying from which district they are. The best example for this is Joopaka Subhadra's short fiction that is based on the life of an agricultural class in rural Telangana. It describes a Dalit woman's concern about the changes that the globalization has brought in, destroying the self-sufficiency of the farmer. One of such stories is her 'Rayakka Kaarati' (Letter from Rayakka).

Dalit writers, especially women writers after the 1980s have employed a very deliberate variant of Telugu that emerges from and represents a specific location of the writers based on caste/subcaste, religion, region and class. This choice became all the more political with the Telangana movement that in a sense represented the culmination of several movements and identities into one movement and one identity and yet retained their heterogeneity. Jajula Gowri's novel *Voyinam* describes itself as a Telangana novel. Telangana novel becomes the sub-title of the novel. It is a momentous journey for the women writers from Harijan identity to scheduled caste identity to Dalit identity to Madiga identity to Telangana identity. Except the Harijan identity, Dalit women writers carry the multiple identities with them and choose to describe themselves in specific terms based on their ideological alliances and requirements.

Paula Gunn Allen, in her introduction to *Spider Woman's Granddaughters* says,

When a people has no control over public perceptions of it, when its sense of self is denied at every turn in the books, films, and television and radio shows it is forced to imbibe, it cannot help but falter. But, when its image is shaped by its own people, the hope of survival can be turned into a much greater hope; it can become a hope for life, for vitality, for affirmation.[12]

In a way, Allen's words articulate the situation that led to native[13] writing, its purpose and its results. This can be borrowed to refer to the need to write from a Dalit perspective since it focuses on a similar situation where the struggle for emancipation from slavery, oppression and exploitation has given rise to native literatures which in turn function as a weapon for the movements.

This book attempts to study the emergence of identities of self in the narratives of Dalit women. A Dalit woman's status in society and literature is an important area of study because while Dalits as a community suffer discrimination, the Dalit woman bears an extra burden of gender. She is not free from the pressure of traditions, toil of customs just because she belongs to the Dalit community which is excommunicated from the village to the outskirts. Even in the case of literature, while Dalits complain of their invisibility or misrepresentation in literature, the Dalit woman remains almost invisible and misrepresented even in most of Dalit literature both as a subject as well as a creator.

Hence, the importance of women's voices of a marginalized section that are raised against caste system, class hierarchy as well as patriarchy. These three patterns are interconnected but also work in different combinations. Caste and class, for instance function together as a combination in certain situations while caste and gender might function together in other situations. Caste, gender and class could also come together in certain other situations. Such combinations are revealed in the narratives when we examine the heterogeneous identities of the speakers with their caste identity being the connecting thread. Patricia Hill Collins, referring to Bonnie Thornton Dill's work,[14] discusses Black women's consciousness, which is relevant to the context that this book is focusing on.

While an Afrocentric feminist epistemology reflects elements of epistemologies used by Africans and women as groups, it also paradoxically demonstrates features that may be unique to Black women. On certain dimensions Black women may more closely resemble Black women, on others, white women; and on still others Black women may stand apart from both groups. Black women's both/and conceptual orientation, the act of being simultaneously a member of a group and yet standing apart from it, forms an integral part of Black women's consciousness. Black women negotiate these contradictions by using this both/and conceptual orientation.[15]

While literatures of the marginalized all over the world emphasize the importance of 'colonized' people rewriting their stories and histories and refusing to remain mere objects of dominant narratives, Dalit women add one more strand to this desire to be the creator, and not remain a mere object, used and misused. So, the portrayal of themselves by Dalit women is the concern of this project in order to understand their perception of their identities. There will be references to the movement, identity politics and literature but the major focus will be on the field work that was done more than a decade ago situated in that particular context.

Dalit writers have repeatedly said that all women are not the same/equal. Depending on caste, class, religion and various other factors, gender is negotiated differently. But, all this is with regard to the women who are aware of Dalit politics and Dalit movement. What about Dalit women who are unaware of all these developments and away from the fruits of the same? The oral narratives clearly show the perspective and perception of Dalit women who are away from all this. They also clearly show how internal hierarchies are carefully preserved not just politically but also socially and culturally. For instance, the stories of Chindu, Dakkali women reveal that they are untouchables not only to the rest of the society but also to Madigas who have played a major role in the Dalit movement. They accept this hierarchy with minimum questioning as the dependent castes of Madigas by tradition.

Thus, Dalit women bring different identities, different situations and different concerns into the picture. The Dalit woman could be anybody ranging from a *jogini* to Dakkali Lachchavva to politician Sadalakshmi. Depending on her specific location, her identity may vary. But the label of untouchability that the society has given her does not change. This project tries to capture the reminiscences of these women about themselves, thus articulating different voices. While Dalit Literature in other languages like Marathi has autobiographies and life stories pouring out and other marginalized writing across the world also show a similar trend, Dalit Literature in Telugu has somehow still not accommodated autobiographies to the extent it can and it has to. Autobiographies are not only important to share one's life stories, as Harriet Jacobs says in her autobiography *Incidents in the Life of a Slave Girl*,[16] but also to make others articulate their experiences. There are many more dimensions of Dalit experience that are yet to find their place in the published Dalit literature. This will happen only when oral narratives and life stories of Dalits are recorded and published, along with the traditional art forms. While the traditional art forms construct a cultural history of Dalits, life stories will construct social histories that can function as documents of experience. Published Dalit women's writing has brilliantly focused on various aspects of Dalit life. But, still some of the areas remain unexplored and unrepresented. The Dalit woman who cannot write or who does not write—her voice is equally important; probably more important because she is placed many steps lower in hierarchy and still has not come out of the burden of silence. That is why this project chose to record and analyse the narratives of Dalit women who have not chosen to write.

The personal narratives included in this project present different aspects of Dalit women's experiences. These women come from different situations and backgrounds. They talk about different issues with different emphases. But, all these reflect the sensibilities of Dalit women. At the same time, this project does not make an attempt to homogenize Dalit women. Although this study is not merely a comparative study of Dalit women's published narratives and oral narratives, comparison does become inevitable in the analysis given their nature of emergence from different contexts and reflection of different aspects of Dalit women's experience and consciousness. With all these differences, Dalit women question society and institutions, and revolt in every possible manner and declare their struggle for freedom. The concept of Double Consciousness that is discussed in the feminist and the black feminist contexts becomes very relevant to theorize the connection between consciousness and experience in the case of Dalit women. Double consciousness emerges from the dual location of women/black women within and outside society, literal and accepted locations respectively, which leads to their understanding of themselves as well as their other.[17] Taking this point a little further, we could say that Dalit women's diverse identities and their experiences lead to their multiple consciousness.

The identities of Dalit women who 'write' and who 'do not write' are different or are presented differently. The differences could be in education, social status, self-sufficiency, rural and urban location, purpose of their writing/not writing, ideologies and movements they are associated with, their professions, economic status, age and others. These differences contribute to the way in which they express themselves/ construct their identities.

In the case of women who do not write, there seems to be a strong wish for education. There is a firm belief that education can prove a source of emancipation for them and people like them. There is a strong desire to change their status and 'rewrite' their stories with the help of education.[18] Education is their redemption and in fact, there is a demand for better schools and better facilities. Most of the Dalit women writers are well-educated and are in privileged positions. Education, obviously, is one of the reasons for their elevated social status and the activity of writing itself. They do not seem to negate this. But, at the same time, they do not seem to believe that education alone can be redemption. They attempt to convey how education has not really changed their identity as 'untouchable women' in society in spite of their privileged positions. For them, a material elevation in their status is not the be all and end all and it cannot really achieve the dignity that they are fighting for in society.

The very act of writing raises several questions as to why they are writing. Is this expression meant for self-assertion or self-construction or self-negation? If they are constructing a self, what kind of a self they construct and how? Obviously, they are trying to break the stereotypes that the dominant society has been imposing on them for ages. How do they break the stereotypes? By proving that the society is wrong or by reiterating what the society thinks about them or by trying to construct what they think they are irrespective of what the society thinks about them? All the above three happen in different contexts, sometimes in the same context. This happens when they construct their identities on their own terms and their people in whom they see themselves and women like them. They write about what they are deprived of and about what they cherish to achieve. These aspects of past, present and future hold a mirror to the life they have led, are leading and the one they dream of. Whether their dreams are fulfilled or shattered, they reflect their idea of their identity and their hopes and aspirations for their future.

The powerful emphasis on self-identity emerges from the treatment that one receives from society and also from one's identity that carries with it centuries of the social history of a country. If self-identity becomes the centre of most Dalit writing, writing self is what Dalit women are doing in their writings. Then, what happens to oral tales where women do not talk, or do not want to talk about themselves? Expression of the self becomes difficult there for there might be restrictions imposed by the caste/village/class bodies. On the other hand, a woman who does not write tries to suppress the fact that people like her are being discriminated against every minute in the society. It could be the sense of self-respect or fear of humiliation that may be guiding her. Everything is alright, everybody is good to them and no problems at all—this seems to be what she says. But, can problems alone be the issue of a text? Is it the politics of discrete/hiding/selective narration that happens in this case? This seems to be the most important difference between Dalit women who write and those who do not. One wants to assert oneself by narrating her marginalized caste status in society. In the case of oral narratives, women do not even want to acknowledge the fact of their 'untouchability' but hide their identity as one that is looked down upon.

While constructing personal and personalized identities in the oral narratives, caste comes into picture only when something specifically related to caste happens. Gender is an oft-discussed issue since most of their problems and concerns are related to their gender identity. Since most of these narratives are collected from women of rural areas, their perspective of life and politics is very different from that of the writers who have published and created a space in public domain by sharing their personal life. The oral narratives also present women who are very much part of their public domain, have a strong sense of the personal, but fail to or rather do not intend to create a space of their own either in the private sphere or in the public sphere. The writers talk about the issue of their acceptability in society whereas the speakers talk about their life and livelihood. Acceptability comes next for them while survival comes first.

They reluctantly accept the status and roles inflicted on them and carry them forward. They may not even refer to the burden of such identities. Two such examples from the narratives that this book focuses on are the schoolteacher and the *jogini* woman. The schoolteacher is aware of the fact that people's attitudes towards her change when they know about her identity. But, she says she has not faced caste discrimination. She in fact tries to cite instances when she was accepted by the mainstream as a student, as a teacher and as a colleague. It is only much later in her narrative that she admits to have faced discrimination based on her caste identity. Similarly, the *jogini* woman says that she was made into a *jogini* when she was a child. If it was later, she would have protested and would have studied. But, she does not say how she protested once she came to know about the exploitation she was subjected to as an adult. Dalit women, in their writings and in their narratives, negotiate locating themselves in a marginal space, sometimes addressing themselves and their people and some other times the others. Bell Hooks' words come very close to Dalit women's resistance when she says,

I am located in the margin. I make a definite distinction between that marginality which is imposed by oppressive structures and that marginality one chooses as site of resistance—as location of radical openness and possibility. This site of resistance is continually formed in that segregated culture of opposition that is our critical response to domination. We come to this space through suffering and pain, through struggle. We know struggle to be that which pleasures, delights, and fulfils desire. We are transformed, individually, collectively, as we make radical creative space which affirms and sustains our subjectivity, which gives us a new location from which to articulate our sense of the world.[19]

The narratives on which this study is based do not reveal a pathetic portrayal or self-pity. Self-respect seems to be guiding them always. Life is a battle for them every moment, every step. They face it like that and are ready to face it like that. Whatever they speak, their focus is on livelihood. Their concept of caste, class, gender and other issues revolve around their livelihood. Although most of them revolt against the

31

system and question the society, they are very keen on marriage and family. They strive hard to support the family and readily accept the responsibility. Their lack of education and political background/exposure turn them into pawns in the power game of politics. Some of them are aware of it and some of them are not. But, they are in a vulnerable and dangerous position. Government accommodates them in the political system only in token. Some of the questions that these women raise and statements they make about their life against society are capable of shaking the foundations of institutions:

1. I don't want to be with the man who is older than me and the man whom I don't like. I wanted to go away with this man. So, I went away. What is wrong?
2. Who will look after me? My family has given me up. If I cease to be a *jogini*, how will I live? Will you provide me livelihood?
3. We (Dalit women) proved that cotton crop does not really require adolescent girls as the tradition makes us believe.

Wendy Singer, in *Creating Histories: Oral Narratives and the Politics of History-Making*,[20] talks about the issue of orality as politics. That way the politics that decides the identity and the politics that is involved in orality are closely linked to each other. The oral narratives of Dalit women that this project deals with also prove this. These narratives may not be deliberately creating history. They may not be recording or recollecting any movement, especially caste, gender or political movements like the book *Manaku Teliyani Mana Charitra* (*We Were Making History*)[21] does. Most of the women interviewed here are not exposed to movements and political ideologies. Hence, there is no deliberate attempt to construct histories and shatter hegemonies. But, their narratives do construct their identities as they perceive themselves or as they want to be perceived by society. While doing so certain facts are revealed, certain realities are concealed, certain expectations are expressed and certain negotiations are initiated.

The most impressive aspect of Dalit women's voices is their courage. Astonishing courage leads them to face life, take up adventures and prove themselves, above all to announce their decisions. A Dalit woman who deserted her husband and went away with another man declares boldly that she does not like her husband because he is old. She may be fined, punished, but she will remain with the second man. Also, some of them negotiate their sexuality in a very frank and bold manner.

Another instance of adventure and experiment is Dalit women successfully experimenting with cotton crop in Maha-bubnagar district. It is a long tradition and belief that only young girls who have not attained puberty should be employed to pluck cotton. One can understand the politics behind it—that of employing children as labourers who will be paid less and made to work more. Dalit women in that village protested against it and took a decision that they will prove how to cultivate cotton crops without employing young girls. They proved it successfully too. This is what characterizes their life and sense of self despite all problems and challenges. Devoid of glorification and romanticization, Dalit women speak of the sordid realities and yet retain their confidence and self-esteem. Their life which is full of song and traditional art forms itself holds a mirror to this.

Challapalli Swarooparani rightly points out that, 'Those who are rejected, need identity. But my understanding is that identity is not everything. Dalit women have to fight not only against the problem of identity but also against all forms of exploitation that they are subjected to in a classist, casteist and patriarchal system.'[22] The latter chapters of this book discuss how the select narratives of Dalit women voice their constant struggle against all forms of exploitation.

NOTES

1. Richard Jenkins, *Social Identity,* London: Routledge, 1996.

2. Toril Moi. 'What is a Woman?', in *What is a Woman and Other Essays,* New York: Oxford University Press, 2001.

3. Iris Marion Young, *On Female Body Experience: 'Throwing Like a Girl' and Other Essays,* New York: Oxford University Press, 2005, p. 25.

4. Anupama Rao, *The Caste Question: Dalits and the Politics of Modern India,* Ranikhet: Permanent Black, 2010, pp. 15–16.

5. Gopal Guru, 'The Language of Dalit-Bahujan Political Discourse', in *Dalit Identity and Politics,* ed. Ghanshyam Shah, New Delhi: Sage Publications, 2001, p. 107.

6. K.S. Singh, ed., *People of India: Andhra Pradesh,* vol. XIII, pt. 1, New Delhi: Affiliated East-West Press Pvt. Ltd., 2003, p. XXX.

7. T.R. Singh, *The Madiga: A Study in Social Structure and Change,* Lucknow: Ethnographic and Folk Cultural Society, 1969.

8. N. Sudhakar Rao, 'The Structure of South Indian Untouchable Castes: A View', in *Dalit Identity and Politics,* ed. Ghanshyam Shah, New Delhi: Sage Publications, 2001, pp. 74–96.

9. Darla Venkateswarrao, *Dalita Sahityam: Madiga Drikpatham (Sahitya Vimarsa Vyasalu),* Hyderabad: Dandora Prachuranalu, 2009.

10. Yendluri Sudhakar, *Vargeekaraneeyam* (Dalita Deergha Kaavyam), Rajahmundry: Manasa and Manogna Prachuranalu, 2004.

11. Joopaka Subhadra and Gogu Shyamala, *Nallaregatisallu: Madiga Upakulala Adolla Kathalu,* Hyderabad: Mysavva Publications, 2006.

12. Paula Gunn Allen, *Spider Woman's Granddaughters: Traditional Tales and Contemporary Writing by Native American Women,* Fawcett Columbine, 1990, pp. 17–18.

13. Paula Gunn Allen is a Native American writer. Native American or American Indians or First Nations are the original inhabitants of Americas who were massacred, subjugated and exploited by the white colonizers.

14. Bonnie Thornton Dill, 'The Dialectics of Black Womanhood', *Signs,* vol. 4, no. 3, Spring 1979, pp. 543–55.

15. Patricia Hill Collins, 'Towards an Afrocentric Feminist Epistemology', in *Feminisms,* ed. Sandra Kemp and Judith Squares, Oxford: Oxford University Press, 1997, pp. 198–205, quoted from http://www.woldww.net/classes/Principles-of-Inquiry/Collins-Afroc FemEpistemology+.htm.

16. Harriet Jacobs aka Linda Brent, *Incidents in the Life of a Slave Girl: Written by Herself*, ed. L. Maria Child, Boston: Published for the Author, 1861.

17. Abigail Brooks, 'Feminist Standpoint Epistemology: Building Knowledge and Empowerment through Women's Lived Experience', in *Feminist Research Practice: A Primer*, ed. Sharlene Nagy Hesse-Biber and Patricia Lina Leavy, Thousand Oaks: Sage Publications, Inc., 2007, pp. 53–82.

18. Most villages in Telangana show an increase in the rate of school-going Dalit children. It could be due to various other reasons also like upper caste children moving towards private schools or urban residential schools, etc. But, the fact is also that there is a strong determination to get educated, with a few examples of Dalits who have reached heights with the help of education.

19. Bell Hooks, 'Choosing the Margin as a Space of Radical Openness', in *The Feminist Standpoint Theory Reader: Intellectual and Political Controversies*, ed. Sandra G. Harding, New York: Routledge, 2004.

20. Wendy Singer, *Creating Histories: Oral Narratives and the Politics of History-Making*, Delhi: Oxford University Press, 1997, p. 159.

21. K. Lalitha et al., eds., *Manaku Teliyani Mana Charitra: Telangana Raitanga Poratamlo Strilu*, Hyderabad: Navayuga Book House, 1986.

22. Challapalli Swarooparani, *Asthitva Gaanam: A Collection of Essays*, Vijayawada: Mythri Prachuranalu 2012, p. 4.

3

Questions of Methodology

As a researcher, teacher and translator in the areas of Australian Aboriginal women's writing, Native Canadian women's writing and Dalit women's writing, I felt that it was important for me to consolidate my understanding of the identity politics to interact with Dalit women who are neither recognized nor commended but lead very 'ordinary' lives in a politically vibrant region like Telangana which has been battling against the political, cultural, economic and social problems. Listening to them has been a great learning and redeeming experience.

Culturally, politically and historically Telangana has been a uniquely located area. It has witnessed many upheavals, atrocities, movements and hardships. While Nizam's rule pushed it into the hands of feudalism, post-independence era has only inflicted the state negligence on it. As a result of this, Telangana has gone through Police Action, Razakar Movement, Telangana Movement and many other revolts. A major influence has been the Naxalite Movement which has its stronghold in Telangana.

Against this background, it is very inspiring to look at the emerging lives and identities of Dalit women in Telangana. Have all these regimes and movements subjugated Dalit women much more or contributed to an awareness among them? How did their caste identities and self-evaluations change? How did the ever-haunting fear of life make them conscious of hierarchies and traditions? Does their conditioned life make them much more hierarchical or give them wings to fly into the sky of progress and equality? Or, has it contributed to a much more careful preservation of traditions and cultures that prove suppressive and oppressive to Dalit women? How far does this 'political' consciousness contribute to the evolution of Dalit women in Telangana?

This project is not about the participants of movements such as *We Were Making History*[1] or *We Also Made History*.[2] The first one records the unheard voices of a movement that has gone into the history of the state but has not included women's voices in its articulation. It excavates the history of the movement from a gender perspective. Women of different castes and ideologies who played an instrumental role in that movement come alive through their narratives recollecting their adventures and grievances. It was a point in the history of movements that the book recorded and so it became an alternative history. Similarly, influenced by this book, Urmila Pawar and Meenakshi Moon edited the latter book incorporating the voices of women from the Dalit movement under the leadership of Dr B.R. Ambedkar. This book not only re-visited the movement but also focused on women's participation in a movement that was always looked upon as Dalit movement basically referring to Dalit men. It succeeds in recording the origins of Dalit women's consciousness by including Mukta Salve's article from the late nineteenth century.

This project is not like Urvashi Butalia's *The Other Side of Silence*[3] or *Speaking Peace*[4] which record the absent women in the documents of violence of the conflict times. Whether it was Punjab and Bengal of the partition times or Kashmir of post-independence India, women's bodies and lives have been the chosen sites of violence. This gendered violence is hardly recorded in history which looks upon the events as the national history or the anti-national history where only the identity of a citizen matters which is quite often that of a male.

This project is neither about success nor about failure, neither about war nor about peace, neither about movement nor about non-movement—but it is about the everyday life of Dalit women. Fifty Dalit women from different communities and backgrounds in various towns and villages of the districts of Mahabubnagar, Ranga Reddy, Hyderabad, Medak, Nalgonda and Warangal have been interviewed. These 50 Dalit women included women from different economic and occupational backgrounds and of different age groups. Some of them were teachers, some were elected people's representatives, some were *joginis*, some were performing Chindu women, some were activists fighting for their people and some without any descriptions and titles. However, they are all unique in their own situations—a revolting *jogini*, a thoughtful teacher, a questioning 'witch', so on and so forth.

This research has not employed a questionnaire but has employed a request that is, 'speak about yourself'. Minimum interference with their narration was the policy that I adopted though I had to pitch in with a few supplementary questions. But, all these were carefully framed so as not to mould the narratives of the speakers. There were no preconceived questions since I strongly believe that spontaneous reactions are more important and construct identities based on their conscious and subconscious concept of self. Probably spontaneity is one factor that marks the major difference between published texts and oral narratives._Not using probes, leading questions and editing elicited unstructured and non–linear narratives from the speakers. They moved back and forth in memory and narrated in a conversational mode in the language that they use in their everyday life. All these factors strengthen the effectiveness of spontaneous narratives in feminist research and help in moving towards strong objectivity and strong reflexivity.

All these 50 narratives form the backdrop of the discussion in this book while twelve of them form the core of the discussion. I have to confess here that the narratives do not represent Dalit women belonging to all sections and all occupations. This is the major limitation of this study. I really thank all the women who readily shared their experiences with me. But, what was most painful was that they all had their own problems which required immediate solutions and they were desperately looking for help. They took me for somebody who could help them and represent their problems. Unfortunately, I could not solve their problems except recording them for an analysis as a researcher and of course empathizing with them. Probably this is one of the most traumatic issues that a researcher faces when one steps into an area like this. Apart from several traps that the feminist ethnography warns the researchers against, such as locating oneself in the field, moving too close to the researched and so on, the field circumstances mentioned above could also throw a trap in front of the researcher of presenting the researched as 'helpless, pathetic, suffering victims without any agency'.

Another factor that decided the narratives that needs to be discussed is the question of privacy. Even as the speaker was discussing the most intimate issues, there was nothing called privacy available to her. Either family or community was always with her, quite often posing questions on behalf of the interviewer or speaking on behalf of the speaker. Thus, apart from the other constraints that these women had, this censorship also moulded these narratives to a great extent making the speaker's role questionable. Like Dalit women's writing being decided by many publishing and readership factors, the oral narratives are also affected by the above factors. Sometimes, as the woman was speaking, family disputes surfaced and sometimes political prejudices.

Sumitra Bhave's book *Pan on Fire: Eight Dalit Women Tell Their Story*[5] in its Introduction raises very important questions about documenting of Dalit women's narratives. I propose to discuss these issues to connect them to the methodological and ideological questions that my research has faced and addressed. Sumitra Bhave says in her Introduction,

This research project is an attempt to find out a woman's image of herself. It is an attempt to see what she sees herself as. She faces life on many fronts, performs many functions and acts in many roles while working out many relationships. We decided to study her in her varied roles to see if we could get at this inner image. The women we studied were divided into four groups: illiterate rural women, highly educated women in industrialized urban areas, Christian members of *secular institutes* and *Dalit* women from city slums.[6]

This book is also an attempt to study the self-image of Dalit women. However, it does not attempt to scrutinize Dalit women in their various roles and functions. It rather goes by the self-description of Dalit women. The women who were interviewed were not divided into any categories since the whole purpose of this project is not to divide Dalit women under categories but to study their concept of their identity given the differences and similarities between them. The location of the Dalit women spoken to also was not radically different as they were located either in villages or in small towns.

Sumitra Bhave goes on to say that,

The method of 'dialogical research' is called so because of the significant characteristics involved in practice. It did not involve an 'interview' but a true 'dialogue'. Whichever questions a woman was expected to answer, were the questions which she, in turn, could ask the investigator and the lives of both were open to each other. In other kinds of research the respondent is mainly a subject of research but here she was much more a participant than a subject. The areas of our lives in which they displayed curiosity guided us to inquire into the same areas in their lives. Thus the investigator too, became more a participant, re-examining her own life through the eyes of the subject investigation.[7]

This observation points to collaborative participatory feminist ethnography where the hierarchy between the researched and the researcher is demolished and shared and combined knowledge systems emerge from the interactions. It is not only learning but also re-discovering of the researcher through the eyes of the researched. The dialogical research puts the researcher and the researched on the same platform for mutual learning. Acceptance of the curiosity of the researched to know about the researcher is a crucial turning point in any research project as it contributes to knowing the researched more and understanding her not only through her answers to the given questions but through her questions expecting answers from the researched. This is the method that this book has followed as well by not only getting information from the women but also answering the questions they asked of the researcher.

However, Frances Maria Yasus, in her Preface to the Book, says,

In her specific role as wife, the *Dalit* woman, in these oral histories, feels a complete failure, as its fulfillment requires reciprocity from her husband, which he does not give. He does not see her as a person, but only as a woman in a prescribed role in which she performs certain prescribed duties, largely as an object of sex. Her feelings of humiliation in having to subject her body and mind to her husband leave a permanent scar on her psyche. Most of the *Dalit* women studied here, appear to hate sex. A man's 'untouchable' sex urge is proof of his manliness and so it does not occur to him to exercise control. Women recognize it and use it as a part of the power game; while men use sex as exploitative power, women use it as manipulative power.[8]

This is an interesting observation about the sexuality of Dalit women and their sexuality as their agency, because she says that Dalit women hate sex due to their frustrating experiences with their men and yet use sex as their manipulative power while men use it as their exploitative power. Is this to say that their sexuality becomes their agency or to say that they use their body as their final resort? Some of the narratives that this book has collected have a reference to their sexual relationships and sexualities. However, they bring them into discussion along with social and cultural issues. Dalit women's sexuality is taken for granted by society and tradition, as has been narrated in Dalit women's writing, but the instance mentioned above reveals how Dalit women could subvert the authority on their sexuality and take it into their control.

Another work that I would like to refer to for a discussion on methodology is *Journeys to Freedom: Dalit Narratives*.[9] The Preface confesses 'We are aware that the study proves little that is conclusive; there is no magical subliminal truth to be uncovered in the lives here recorded. The capacity for remembering and the highlighting of certain details rather than others sheds light on identities shaped by materials as well as non-material factors';[10] and says at a later point,

memory is a key to identifying the important elements in a life. Only that is remembered which impinged, however apparently irrelevant the detail; and that which impinged must have done something in the person, thereby determining identity. On the question of whether personal recollection can be made the ground of social meaning, we maintain ... that the form of the narrative chosen reveals identity-building experience and a world-view, and that tone of voice and choice of words reveal the person.[11]

This book will also attempt to analyse how the selective memory and use of language, repetitions, assertions and questions give clues to the chosen profiling of Dalit women. This analysis functions as the most crucial point of understanding of the subversions of the inflicted images and stereotypes on these women.

NOTES

1. K. Lalitha et al., eds., *Manaku Teliyani Mana Charitra: Telengana Raitanga Poratamlo Strilu*, Hyderabad: Navayuga Book House, 1986.
2. Urmila Pawar and Meenakshi Moon, eds., Wandana Sonalkar, tr., *We also Made History: Women in the Ambedkarite Movement*, New Delhi: Zubaan, 2008.
3. Urvashi Butalia, *The Other Side of Silence: Voices from the Partition of India*, Durham: Duke University Press, 2000.
4. Urvashi Butalia, ed., *Speaking Peace: Women's Voices from Kashmir*, New Delhi: Kali for Women, 2002.
5. Sumitra Bhave, *Pan on Fire: Eight Dalit Women Tell Their Story*, tr. Gauri Deshpande, New Delhi: Indian Social Institute, 1998.
6. Ibid., Introduction, p. xvii.
7. Ibid., p. xiii.
8. Ibid., Preface, p. xiii.
9. Fernando Franco, Jyotsna Macwan and Suguna Ramanathan, *Journeys to Freedom: Dalit Narratives*, Kolkata: Stree Samya, 2004.
10. Ibid., Preface, p. viii.
11. Ibid., p. 3.

4

Dalit Feminist Ideology

GOGU SHYAMALA, IN an interview, identifies herself as a Dalit Feminist and also defines Dalit Feminism. She says,

I would like to be identified as a Dalit feminist writer since it is from the perspective of Dalit feminism only that we can understand anything, and question everything. And for us, there are no limitations in this kind of framework: such a Dalit Feminist perspective is all about self-respect and women's assertion. It is through such assertion and self-respect only we claim our Dalit identity; only after the consciousness we have gained from the struggles against untouchability and discriminations in varied forms.[1]

Joopaka Subhadra, in her editorial introduction to *Nallaregati Sallu* conceptualizes the identity of the Madiga subcaste women based on the difference between them and the other women. In order to establish this difference, she chooses to subvert history from a Dalit woman's perspective, to be precise, from a Madiga woman's perspective. She argues that Madiga and

Madiga subcaste women cultivated the land, tamed the buffaloes for agriculture, practiced medicine and untiringly spread the art forms and that women of other castes learnt these skills, knowledge and art forms from the Madiga women. She asserts that it is no longer the stories of Rama and Krishna that need to be narrated but the stories of Ekalavya whose thumb was cut off, Shambuka whose head was severed, Surpanakha whose nose and ears were mutilated, Tataki who was killed and Yellamma who remained a mere torso. Subhadra cites the example of African–American women and states that like the white women appropriating feminism in Europe, upper caste women in India have taken feminism into their control. She elucidates how caste in this country is not allowing women to come together in solidarity. Like 'Alisamma Women's Collective', Subhadra also presents the oppositional binary of upper caste and lower caste women created by society. This binary leads towards Subhadra's assertion of Madiga woman's unique and self-sufficient existence. In her editorial introduction to *Nallaregati Sallu,* Subhadra argues that caste is preventing women of this country from uniting as one. She says that upper caste women are politely insulted while the lower caste women are harshly insulted. Upper caste women are made into housewives and *grihalakshmis* and imprisoned within the four walls of home while the lower caste women are made into servants working outside day and night. Upper caste women are made into family women while lower caste women into prostitutes, *joginis* and *basivis* (*Dalit devadasis*). They are invited into education and employment while the latter are pushed into hunger and poverty. Here is an argument that emphasizes the differences, calls for solidarity and identifies caste as a major obstacle for women's solidarity. She says,

Those who do not fit into the morals that does not matter if the life is lost but modesty should not be lost; those who do not care for the feudal values of the husband being equal to the visible god; those who possess the natural human values and do not get burnt on

45

the husband's funeral pyre; those who have the right and the guts to sit along with men in the panchayats; those who have not yet been able to get rid of the birthing smell of matriarchy; those who carry the burden of family on their heads; those who are doing unending bonded labour at home and outside—Madiga subcaste women.[2]

She argues that all women have to recognize the political importance of this difference between Madiga women and other women and reminds that the caste relationships inherent in gender, class and caste constructions should be democratized. She points out how feminists did not grieve about the insult and injustice that Surpanakha, Tataki and Yellamma were subjected to as much as they did about the injustice to which the women such as Sita, Savitri, Anasuya and Ahalya were subjected to. She traces the reason for this difference in their reaction to caste that influenced them not to discuss this issue in depth. She continues to say that the unfortunate aspect of identity movements is the inability to get rid of the wicked political strategies that look down upon the lower castes. She emphatically states that the upper caste feminists' parameters will be inadequate to measure the lower caste women's problems. She goes on to say that neither in literature nor in reform movement did lower caste women find a place. She raises a pertinent question as to why 'untouchable' women have to carry on their shoulders the social reformers who strived for the betterment of upper caste women and spread upper caste values in the name of women's emancipation and social reform.

Sharmila Rege, a renowned non-Dalit scholar of Dalit writings/studies in her article 'Dalit Women Talk Differently' says that 'the assertion of Dalit women's voices is not just an issue of naming their "difference". "Naming of difference" leads to a narrow identitarian politics—rather this assertion is read as a centring of the discourse on caste and gender and is viewed as suggesting a dalit feminist standpoint.'[3] It is this Dalit feminist standpoint that Joopaka Subhadra is discussing above.

It is not just to say that there is difference between Dalit and non-Dalit women but also to unravel the ways of understanding this difference in order to dismantle the patriarchal and feudal casteist structures that women are ruled by. Sharmila Rege's article was a response to Gopal Guru's article on Dalit women talking differently from other women. While Gopal Guru proves in his argument as to how Dalit women talk differently, Sharmila Rege agrees that they talk differently, and that the Dalit women do talk about the difference. However, she strongly argues that listing out of the differences in itself is not sufficient to establish a Dalit feminist perspective.

Challapalli Swarooparani attempts to identify the roots of Dalit Feminism. In the process she acknowledges the great thinkers from the Dalit and non-Brahmin, Dravidian movements as the inspiring pioneers of Dalit feminism. She says,

Elimination of caste system and action against Hindu ideology as formulated by the Dalit philosophers Phule, Periyar, Ambedkar and Bhagya Reddy Varma is the foundation for Dalit feminism. The Dalit woman totally opposes all kinds of evils in this system such as caste, religious fundamentalism and classist exploitation. That the emancipation of the exploited is not possible without questioning the caste discrimination, gender discrimination, upper caste feudal domination and labour exploitation rooted in layers against the Dalit women in the Indian casteist and classist society is the Dalit feminist ideology.[4]

This argument takes the feminist ideology beyond the concept of gender and extends its concern for the other categories of people who are marginalized. It brings together the categories like caste, class, gender, occupation, region and religion in the Indian society.

Swarooparani convincingly traces the origins of Dalit Feminist thought to the stalwarts of lower caste movements. Let us also see how the contemporary Dalit Feminist argument began. Dalit women students of University of Hyderabad published a 'Statement of Dalit Women' on 8 March, the International Women's Day in 2002. It was signed by Swathy Margaret, Jalli India and others. This statement addressed the upper caste women as sisters and argued how all women have to come together to understand the oppression that they are subjected to by the casteist patriarchal society. 'We, Dalit women want Hindu women and other non-Dalit women to recognize that Indian female community is stratified by casteist patriarchal system. Caste system, both as hegemony and political structure works against the unity of Indian women. For centuries this scene is not altered.'[5] The group called itself Alisamma Women's Collective after the Dalit woman Alisamma who was subjected to violence in Dalit-non-Dalit conflict. This statement was also called Dalit Feminist Manifesto after the Black Feminist Manifesto.

The statement is addressing the non-Dalit women, not to blame them or declare a war against them but to convince them to understand the intricacies of the caste system. Like Joopaka Subhadra and Challapalli Swarooparani and other Dalit women writers, this statement is also emphasizing the difference between them and the others. However, like Sharmila Rege argues, they are also able to explain the difference as a critical category that can bring about solidarity between the sections of women subjected to marginalization, though divided by differences. It is an attempt to form an alliance against the feudal, hierarchical system perpetrated by the Manuvadis. Most importantly, it is a sisterhood based on awareness and transformation that they are arguing for.

Dr B.R. Ambedkar in his pioneering article addressed to the high caste Hindu women[6] unveils the politics of distrust, suspicion, discrimination and ill-treatment that was nurtured against the Hindu women by the Hindu scriptures. He compares this conspiracy of Manudharma against Hindu women with that of its design against the Dalits. Thus, a parallel is established for possibilities of self-discovery as well as solidarity based on the differences in status and treatment. Upper caste men, women and Dalit men have attempted to define Dalit women, speak on behalf of them and reform them. But, 'Alisamma Women's Collective' speaks as a Dalit women's collective and calls upon the upper caste women to join in solidarity as all women are subjected to the hegemony of the patriarchal society. The Dalit woman who is made into a site of definitions and reforms by the upper caste men, women and Dalit men, exposes the system and defines the upper caste women in 'Alisamma Women's Collective' by establishing the need for networking of all women. By extending their hand in solidarity, they are taking initiative in formulating alliances against the oppressive forces and are also signalling a mature stage in the movement where not mere slogans but constructive suggestions and solid moves become the strategy. 'That you are made whereas we are mutilated. You are put on a pedestal, whereas we are thrown into fields to work day and night. You were made Satis, we were made harlots.'[7]

Dalit women writers like Vimal Thorat, Baby Kamble, Urmila Pawar and Meenakshi Moon writing in other Indian languages have also repeatedly pointed out that Dalit women's issues have been relegated to the margins by both women's movements, as well as the Dalit movement. In the words of Vimal Thorat, 'We have been kept out, left behind, denied by our own movement (the Dalit movement) and also by the women's movement. Both are cynically quiet when Dalit women, who enter the political space at the panchayat level, are compelled to face acts of brutal humiliation, violation and violence. Why?'[8]

It is from this understanding and angst that the call for solidarity between women of different sections emerges. It is the Dalit women's struggle to get rid of the multiple jeopardy that they are subjected to. They refuse to accept the romanticized portrayal by men of their communities as well as the condemning images perpetrated by the upper caste men and women.[9]

On the other hand, there are Dalit women writers and activists who have argued that solidarity is possible between women of oppressed sections but not between the oppressing and the oppressed sections. Mary Madiga says,

It is the Madiga woman who identifies the tools while sowing. Brahmin women or kamma women have no such experience. Those women do not even come to the fields. It is the Madiga woman who has the experience. It is our woman who tells which is whisk and which is grain.... Clothes will stink without a washerwoman. If there is no Madiga, there will be no death, no marriage. The corpses will not be removed. If there is no barber, the beard will grow, smell dirty and that fellow will be destroyed. Although a barber woman cleans up the dirt and the dirty child, she has no value in this society. Although a washerwoman cleans up the dirt in the whole village, in this society people call her you Lachhi, come here and throw some food at her. That's all, otherwise does she have any value![10]

The terms of solidarity and comparison here are not gender but the hegemony of caste. There is an attempt to build parallels between toiling people who have no value in the society because of their caste and the occupation that is inherited along with their caste identity.

While we are on the subject of Dalit feminism and solidarity, it is only relevant to discuss the recent debates and alliances among the Dalit women writers in Telugu. Women writers in Telugu with different ideologies and from varied backgrounds resolved to form a group after lengthy discussions and deliberations. They called it *Manalo Manam*, among ourselves. This coming together of the women writers marks a milestone as such a gesture of solidarity among women writers has not been witnessed in the history of Telugu literature despite harsh criticism and crude attacks on women writers at various points of time. The first meeting of *Manalo Manam* happened on 11 January 2009 bringing together women writers from the privileged, underprivileged, minority, traditional and radical sections and ideologies. The meeting witnessed differences emerging from the diverse identities of these women writers. The second meeting on 22 March 2009 gave rise to the emergence of a parallel group called *Mattipulu*, Flowers of the Soil, with the Dalit, tribal, backward caste and minority women writers. Joopaka Subhadra one of the founder members of *Mattipulu* looks upon it not as a group taking birth out of *Manalo Manam* but as a context that has brought together the voices of marginalized women.

Mattipulu, as a forum for women writers of Telugu from the disadvantaged sections functions as a major breakthrough in the identity politics and especially in the debates related to Dalit feminism. It is not only a literary phenomenon but a culmination of cultural, social and political developments that Dalit women have been negotiating with. It is a journey that Dalit women writers have embarked upon from Alisamma Women's Collective when they were convincing the other women for solidarity through *Manalo Manam* when they actually came together to *Mattipulu* where they decided their alliances after experimenting with the combinations of solidarity.

It will be helpful to familiarize ourselves with the resolutions made by *Mattipulu*, an SC, ST, BC, Minority women writers' organization to understand their political positioning and their declaration of their ideologies and choices. This forum will attempt to portray the lives of SC, ST, BC and Minority women in literature.

1. will work against caste and gender hegemony and against all other hegemonies.

2. will support all literary identities.
3. will support separate Telangana and SC categorization.
4. will oppose eviction of tribals in the name of development.
5. will work for separate quota for SC, ST, BC and Minority women in political reservations for women.
6. demands for inclusion of life and culture of labour of SC, ST, BC and Minority sections in curriculum and for deletion from the curriculum of ideas and attitudes that humiliate them.

Mattipulu, as seen above, goes beyond literature, gender and caste in its concerns. It declares solidarity with other marginalized women and also with the boiling political issues such as formation of a separate state of Telangana and the categorization of Dalits. The fact that needs to be kept in mind here is that the women who have come together as *Mattipulu* consisted of all subcastes of Dalit, tribal and backward castes, all religions such as Islam, Christianity, Hinduism and Buddhism, all regions of erstwhile Andhra Pradesh that is Rayalaseema, Telangana and Coastal Andhra and all ideologies including those of the Marxist. Despite their diversity, women of *Mattipulu* were able to empathize with the movements to take a clear political stand.

This story of alliances and solidarities continued with the formation of Democratic Women Writers' Forum with some writers of the marginalized sections and with majority of women writers from the privileged sections. On 8 March 2010, Challapalli Swarooparani and Katyayani Vidmahe announced the formation of Democratic women writers' forum. They described it as a new form of the temporary united women's forum *Manalo Manam*.

It would be interesting to read, in this context, an article on the need to redefine feminism written by M.M. Vinodini. It was published on 22 February 2010, two weeks before the emergence of Democratic Women's Forum. Like the Dalit Feminist Manifesto that gently reminded the upper caste women that they were with upper caste men when the patriarchal, casteist society was victimizing Dalit women, Vinodini also discusses how feminists of the privileged sections share space at home and in society with men who are instrumental in the running of a hierarchical system. She makes it clear that Dalit women had and have no role in formulating oppressive patriarchy against women. So, Dalit women support and respect feminism as an alternative identity movement.

Vinodini raises pertinent questions about feminist movement not declaring solidarity with Dalit movement and reiterates that gender is the only problem for upper caste women while Dalit women have to face problems emerging from their multiple marginalized identities. She suggests that the upper caste women should not stand with the upper caste men in implementing *manuvada*, rather should come down and join the marginalized women in their fight against the oppressive ideology. Challapalli Swarooparani, another Dalit woman writer who was instrumental in forming the Democratic Women Writers' Forum also makes a similar proposition when she says,

In terms of identity, Dalit woman is below the upper caste woman and Dalit man. Standing on the last step of laddered society of this country, lives a miserable life as Dalit among Dalits deprived of any status among women. She faces majorly three kinds of oppression in her daily life. Casteism, class exploitation and male domination are tearing a Dalit woman's life into shreds.[11]

Vinodini attempts to classify Dalit feminist poetry under six major heads based on the themes and concerns of the poetry—Dalit women's toil/slogging/slavery; Dalit women-untouchability; upper caste men's violence/attacks/rapes/killings of Dalit women; upper caste women's authority on Dalit women; Dalit men's authority on Dalit women; Devadasi system.[12]

All these issues are dealt with by most of the Dalit women writers. The narratives of Dalit women that this book is based on, also express their preoccupation with the above issues in different contexts.

Challapalli Swarooparani contradicts the mainstream feminist movements about the origins of feminism and tries to locate the movement in the context of the lower caste women's awareness about their rights. She says,

According to Dalit women scholars, it is not correct to think that feminism started in 1970s in India. In fact, it can be said that the consciousness about women's rights started in this country when Ambedkar established a women's association under his wife Ramabai's leadership in 1920s. There is not much difference between the traditionalists of the Hindu Code Bill times and the present day progressive activists in their attitude. Both are narrow-minded. While the traditionalists in those times thought that the traditional family system will be destroyed if women are given liberty in the issues of marriage, divorce and adoption, those who oppose sub-quota in women's reservation bill are acting with an intention that the rights this bill gives should belong only to their sections.[13]

All these definitions and arguments suggest that Dalit women are not against the concept and ideology of feminism but are against the exclusivist attitude of the feminist movement. That women belonging to the privileged sections were equally colonizing the underprivileged women along with their own women, is the argument that we get to hear from across the world, whether it is is Black or Native or class contexts. Dalit women are also raising a similar question about solidarity between women of all sections. They are addressing the other women but are also stating that even if the other woman sympathizes with them, she continues to be part of the colonizing sections.

Dalit women create the categories such as upper caste men, women and Dalit men—who in turn are the ones that ignore, neglect and oppress Dalit women at various levels. By doing so, they are discussing the layered multiple oppression that Dalit women are subjected to. Patriarchy, both within and without and casteism become two pertinent targets for Dalit women in securely establishing their location as Dalit women.

Jhansi K.V. Kumari, in her essay 'Inner Self', locates the issue of gender in the context of Ambedkarism, thus shifting the concentration from Puranic age to contemporary age. Although she does attack gender discrimination in general, she aims at the patriarchal and male chauvinistic attitude of Dalit men. This connects her arguments with the arguments of Dalit Feminists who juxtapose Dalit women against upper caste men, upper caste women as well as Dalit men. Dalit women declare their belief, support and commitment for the Dalit movement and the inspiration given by Ambedkar. At the same time, they question the gender discrimination within Dalit societies. In fact, Jhansi K.V. Kumari questions the loyalties of Dalit leaders to Dalit movement and the memory of Ambedkar, because Ambedkar strived for the upliftment of Dalit women as well. She says,

Ambedkar was the first person who thought about women's liberty and rights, tried to put them into practice, was victimized by the handcuffs of hatred of Manuvadis and gave up his position. Will people who lecture on his birth anniversary gatherings as his followers ever respect his opinion? Will they put them into practice? Will they go in that direction, in the first place?[14]

To conclude in the words of Gogu Shyamala,

As a Dalit woman where should I fight this patriarchy is the phenomenal question that disturbs every Dalit mind in India today. Since nowadays, the Dora disappeared in the village in the context of globalization, the enemy also seems to be disappeared. The patriarchal symbol 'Husband' too seems to be changing. Today in

India the lands in lakhs of acres are being given to SEZs (Special Economic Zone) instead of Dalits and poor as largesse. Handlooms, cottage and community and village products and utilities have also disappeared from even the very villages and communities once used to be hot beds for the same. Pots are given up almost and plastic pots and utilities have become rampant. Who is the enemy then? Brahmanical Patriarchy has taken the form of capitalism, bureaucracy, judiciary, political parties even socialism and communism ideologies including Naxalism which includes Manu, Landlord, Brahmin, Bania, a Member of Parliament, Legislative Assembly, a Minister or Chief Minister in the Government or a big Contractor or industrialist in the private sector. It is possible to look at it purely from Dalit feminist perspective.[15]

NOTES

1. Gogu Shyamala in Conversation with Rajkumar Eligedi, *Writers in Conversation*, vol. 1, no. 1, February 2014, http://fhrc.flinders.edu. au/writers_in_conversation.
2. Joopaka Subhadra and Gogu Shyamala, *Nallaragatisallu: Madiga Upakulala Adolla Kathalu*, Hyderabad: Mysavva Republications, 2006, p. vii.
3. Sharmila Rege, 'Dalit Women Talk Differently', *Economic and Political Weekly*, 31 October 1998, WS-39.
4. Challapalli Swarooparani, *Asthitva Gaanam: A Collection of Essays*, Vijayavada: Mythri Prachuranalu, 2012, p. 16.
5. Swathy Margaret, et al., 'Statement of Dalit Women', http://mail. sarai.net/pipermail/test1/2002-March/001229.html.
6. Dr B.R. Ambedkar, 'Rise and Fall of Hindu Woman, in *Writings and Speeches of Dr B.R. Ambedkar*, vol. 4, Education Department, Government of Maharashtra, 1987.
7. Swathy Margaret et al., 'Statement of Dalit Women'. http://mail. sarai.net/pipermail/test1/2002-March/001229.html.
8. Vimal Thorat, 'Dalit Women have been Left Behind by the Dalit Movement and the Women's Movement', http://www.sabrang. com/cc/archive/2001/may01/cover1.htm.
9. For more details and discussion, see my article titled 'From Alisamma Women's Collective to Mattipulu', in *Towards Social Change: Essays*

    on Dalit Literature, ed. Sankar Prasad Singha and Indrani Acharya, Hyderabad: Orient BlackSwan, 2014, pp. 159–75.

10. Mary Madiga, *Nallapoddu: Dalit Staila Sahityam 1921–2002*, Hyderabad: Hyderabad Book Trust, 2002, pp. 370–1.

11. Challapalli Swarooparani, *Asthitvaganam*, pp. 7–8.

12. M.M. Vinodini, *Strivada Kavitvam: Bhasha, Vastu, Rupa Naveenatha*, Hyderabad: Hailey Print Media, 2011, p. 266.

13. Challapalli Swarooparani, *Asthitvaganam*, p. 63.

14. Jhansi K.V. Kumari, 'Inner Self', in *Flowering from the Soil: Dalit Women's Writing from Telugu,* tr. and com. K. Suneetha Rani, New Delhi: Prestige Books International, 2012, p. 208.

15. Gogu Shyamala, Interview.

5

Caste and Religion

THIS CHAPTER DISCUSSES the self-introductions of the Dalit women based on their caste and religion. Most of the women started their narratives by introducing themselves by their caste identities. This introduction brought out the identities ranging from the categories to the castes and subcastes. Also, this introduction led to a very clear juxta-position of I/we and they which function not only as binaries but also as opposing binaries. The people juxtaposed could be the neighbourhood people, co-workers, community or the speaker's husband. Such a juxtaposition helps make it clear as to where the speakers locate themselves. I will attempt to examine the self-identification in terms of the caste identity, first.

One woman identifies herself as an SC and locates herself among the landless labouring people. 'We are SCs. We are ordinary labourers. We have some land. We cannot live unless we do some work.' Without any hesitation she identifies herself in constitutional/governmental terms. Quickly after that she also refers to the fact that 'they' don't treat them (her and family/community) well. She asks a pertinent question about the difference by saying that it won't be milk if the upper caste people's bodies are cut and blood if their bodies are cut. Her logic is that if everyone has blood, everyone should be treated equal. Thus, her identification with a governmental category culminates in her identification with her people and recognition of the other sections. She and her people have a caste/category. However, 'they' have no caste or category.

Another woman identifies herself with her subcaste by introducing herself as a Madiga. She says, 'We are Madigas. We are called Madigas.' This is an interesting shift from 'we are' to 'we are called'. Her unhesitating and proud declaration of identity goes on to question the caste discrimination. Like the woman quoted in the above narrative, she too identifies herself with the working people for whom work is everything. Another woman introduces herself as a landless labourer belonging to the Mala caste. A young girl who goes for shepherding introduces herself as Madiga and quickly adds that she is a Harijan. She is quite often abused as a girl, a Dalit and also as a trespasser. She says, 'When I don't have to graze the goats, I work in the fields. When I go with goats, I have to listen to all kinds of things. If the goats enter the fields, the landlords abuse. I feel bad listening to the abuses.' These abuses are hurled at her not only identity as an individual shepherdess but also as a Dalit shepherdess. Similarly, an older woman identifies herself as a Mala and distinguishes between Malas and Madigas. She locates herself clearly in the Mala community. 'They' are addressed as Harijans. Here, her 'other' is not the dominant other, but the other subcaste who is lower to her in the caste stratification. Her emphasis on restrictions on inter-dining and inter-marriage also reiterates the difference:

We don't eat at each other's house. We are not used to it from the beginning. If there is a function in our house, we call them and feed

them. But, we don't go. We are like that from the beginning. We
have no food-alliance, marriage-alliance. We don't marry their girls
and they don't marry our girls. They are Harijans, you know! We are
Malas. We are different, they are different.

On the other hand, Mary Madiga in her narratives asserts
her identity not at the individual level but at the community
level. 'Madigas are the most beautiful people. Madigas are the
strongest people. We are ahead of everything. Although into
physical labour, our children are beautiful. Jealous of this, they
rape our children. Because we are Madigas, they fulfil their
desires and throw us into poverty.'[1] Dakkali Lachhi, whose
surname is her caste name describes in detail as to how they
are dependent on Madigas, 'We beg at Madiga households. We
stay near their houses. We are born to beg from them. We don't
know any other work. Whether they give us or don't give us,
we do just that. We don't ask others. We don't ask other castes
for food and we don't work. We are born like this.' She makes a
very important statement that can sum up the hierarchical caste
system in a few words: 'Madigas give us food and look after us
but they don't touch us. Other castes don't touch Malas and
Madigas. Harijans do not touch us. When we go to beg also
we have to sit at a distance. They give us a quilt made of old
clothes, begging bowl, earthen pot and food'.[2]

Similarly, another Chindu woman intelligently conveys
two important details about the interactions between the Dalit
communities and the satellite communities. One, 'they' live in
big houses and Chindus live outside; Chindus beg and 'they'
give. But, she says, they all live together and Madigas treat
Chindus well. But she concludes her narrative with a rhetorical
question that they don't give even when she begs, will they
give if she doesn't. It speaks volumes about the predicament of
a woman belonging to the lowest strata of the society being
marginalized by the mainstream society as well as the caste they

are dependent on, the caste that stands on the last step of the ladder of caste stratification.

On the other hand, the schoolteacher says that one of her girl students burst out pleading with her not to say that she was an SC: 'Don't say that you are an SC, say that you are a brahmin or a vysya. People said like this near the fields, I fought with them saying that you are not from that caste, don't say like that, say that you are from another caste, to anybody. Those children don't like it.' This is a peculiar situation of having to hide one's identity in order to get a nod of acceptance from the dominant sections. Not only that she is supposed to hide her identity but also has to take on a false identity to become acceptable to the village. It appears as if the girl student was articulating the hidden, repressed anxiety and insecurity that the teacher herself was carrying with her who says that she was treated well as long as her identity was not known but afterwards it changed. When she talks about the caste representations and attitudes prevalent among the school children, that school turns into a miniature of the village. She does not even mention where she would locate herself in the caste dynamics of the village as reflected on the school.

As opposed to this repeated reference to one's caste identity and the questions around it, there are some narratives that do not mention the caste of the speaker. The woman who was beaten up for entering into the temple with the man she was in relationship with does not refer to her caste identity anywhere in her narrative. But, her caste identity is hinted at when she refers to her marriage, village boundaries, response of the outside world and also when she says that they did not enter the inner temple but slept under a tree.

The young girl who migrated to the city as a domestic help also does not refer to her caste. Two major ideas about herself that she has are that she went to work and got education. Her education stopped along with her employment when she went back to her village for a family function. Similarly, the woman who is working to bring the children back home is the one who is subjecting her life and her attitude to a review. There is no reference to her caste identity in her narrative. There is no community affiliation except her identification with children and girls who are deprived of education and are married off at an early age. She refers to the cross-section of students, especially dropouts and child labourers whom they have brought back to education. She says that there are children of all castes among those children including SCs, STs, BCs and OCs, but mostly SCs. She is sensitive and alert to the social identities of these children. But, she does not identify herself with any caste identity. That she is more concerned about her life as changed by early marriage and deprivation of education could be one reason for her identifying herself more with children crushed under the familial responsibilities.

Caste identity cannot be discussed in isolation from religious identities and associations. The women whose narratives are recorded for this book affiliate themselves with Hindu religion. Some women speak how they are not allowed into the temples though they go there with all devotion. Some others say that they do not go to the temple as they are not allowed inside. Some refer to the religious customs that turned them into servants of the temple and the village and yet branded them as 'untouchables'. Some others discuss the laddered caste system and the dependent status of their caste. Some of them also invoke the mythologies to subvert the caste hierarchy and establish the esteem of their caste in their re-tellings.

One woman, who identifies herself as an SC, says that they are not allowed into the temple and are asked to stay away from the temple. They stand outside and offer prayers. Their offerings are accepted from outside but they are not allowed inside: 'However well we are, no matter with how many worships and prayers we go there, they keep us away, they don't allow us'.

This woman locates herself among her people who are made to stand outside the temple reiterating their location outside the village. Similarly, a member of MPTC (Mandal Parishad Territorial Constituencies) who identifies herself as a Madiga, says, 'They invite me into the temple. But, I don't go. I don't feel like going. We can't go. Some people ask us to come in. Some people tell us to stand outside and see. It is like that. None of us go to the temple. We celebrate festivals at home.' She sounds as if she is convincing herself and convincing people around her that she enjoys certain acceptability and status despite which she cannot and does not want to go there due to some other reasons. Suddenly 'I' becomes 'we' when she says 'none of us go to the temple'. Probably here she feels conscious as to how her people are treated as a community and how she is also part of her community when it comes to the question of temple entry.

She shifts between 'I' and 'we'. When she refers to herself in her roles as a wife/mother, she uses I thus making her experience very specific and individualistic and asserting her identity as an individual but not just as a category. When she talks about 'we', she speaks as a member of that family in which nobody has government employment. She becomes a villager who looks forward to the betterment of her village. She takes up the role of a member of Dalit/SC community when she speaks about the welfare/betterment of her village.

One is here reminded of what Anupama Rao says while she is on the subject of temple entry in pre-independence early half of twentieth century,

Temple entry occupied a different position in the Dalit political repertoire. If nationalists framed the temple as an exceptional structure because it was a place of religious worship, Dalit activists equated temples with enclosed public spaces, such as schools, hotels, and teashops, in their bid to clarify the legal principle of equal access. Their politicization of temple entry emphasized the resemblance between the temple and the other public places, thereby refusing the a priori sacrality of the temple. Such a strategy allowed them to make an assault upon one of the most symbolically overdetermined spaces in the Hindu socio-political imaginary through the idiom of equal access, rather than through claims for equality of worship.[3]

While the two women discussed above on one hand say that they want to go and they do go but they are not allowed into the temple as a community, they also state that they don't want to go even if they are allowed inside the temple. Another woman goes to the temple to take blessings for her ailing son but she also turns it into a site where she, her lover and her son could come together. On the other hand, there is a 'Mala' woman who says that they don't do any pujas but sacrifice cattle to their Yellamma goddess on festival days. This also hints at their beliefs and rituals that save them from waiting at the doorstep of the mainstream temple.

One *jogini* woman says that at the age of seven, she was given up for becoming a *jogi*. She is dissociated from her family or rather she is disowned by them. This tradition is like a curse on Dalit girl children. An unaware and uninformed girl child is made into a *jogini*. The mainstream society does not think that her consent is at all important. Family and community are made to follow the orders of the hegemonic structures such as religion, village and society. Their decision becomes binding on Dalit community that results in a family submitting the girl child to the temple to become a Dalit devadasi. Victimized by the tradition, she has to survive on begging. She is deprived of family, education, livelihood, sexual and marital rights. Probably the bar on Dalits from entering the temple also forces them to submit their girl child not only to get an entry into the temple but also to live as the consort of the god/goddess.

This topic has been discussed in depth in Dalit writings as well. Nagappagari Sundarraju's story 'Nadiminti Bodekka Basiviralayyeda'[4] and Gogu Shyamala's short story 'Radam'[5] leave an everlasting impact on the readers with their critical outlook of this oppressive tradition. While Sundarraju's story seems to suggest that this practice is invincible in a rural system, Shyamala's story presents a family's determination to save its daughter from the clutches of the evil tradition even at the cost of losing all that they have and leaving the village with nothing of their own.

Similarly, we come across Chindu women who are per-forming women from dependent castes repeatedly referring to their status as decided by the religion. Tradition makes a Chindu woman survive on begging. Government gave her a house. But, she wants land to cultivate and live on her own. This indicates the desire for occupational mobility. However, she also expresses her helplessness of having to stick to her traditional profession. She says, 'Whatever it is, I have to beg. Touch people's feet, salute their children and beg. I have to give thousand rupees to people to beg in a village. If I get something, I will live. Otherwise, I have to return without saying a word. That is the kind of life this is.'

On the other hand, Dakkali Lachhi, belonging to another dependent subcaste subverts the caste hierarchy by re-telling the origin myths from the point of view of her caste. Like the above-mentioned Chindu woman saying that she pays money to beg in a village, Dakkali Lachhi says that

When our caste was born, Madigas made us sit on the excreta and agreed to give us a quilt made of old clothes, begging bowl and an earthen pot, food grains annually and 10 g. of gold. That is why they give us food. It is our right to beg and their responsibility to give. They are our fathers. We are like their daughters. That is why they don't allow us to leave the village on a Friday.

Lachhavva proudly declares that they beg only from Madigas and that it is their right to beg from them. Dependence turns into right in her narrative.

Mary Madiga also chooses a myth to establish the greatness of Madiga women. She retells the story of Arundhati from a Madiga woman's perspective. A brahmin was looking for a worthy woman who can boil the pebbles. He could not find one like that anywhere. Finally, he went to Madiga households. Arundhati, on the orders of Jambavanta boiled the pebbles to prove the greatness of Madigas, especially the chastity and devotion of Madiga women. Mary takes this episode to establish relations between upper castes and lower castes. According to her, brahmins and kshatriyas are Arundhati's children. So, the brahmin who married Arundhati is the brother-in-law of Madigas.

In continuation to this discussion, it will be interesting to read how Swarooparani uses different symbols to portray Dalit women in her poetry. Her poem 'Mankenapoovu'[6] presents various shades of a Dalit woman's identity. She is a wriggling *palapitta* (blue jay) caught in a thorny bush. Thorns are the handcuffs of slavery layered around her for ages. Her gender consciousness overtly speaks to the readers as to how she is marginalized as a woman and as a Dalit woman. As a Dalit woman, her position becomes much more delicate as the society assumes that Dalit women are easily available. It is male chauvinism and caste hegemony, the double bind of hierarchy that haunts her and subjugates her. She presents herself as an object of desire, as a subject for violence, as a butt of insult, as a target of discrimination. She feels like sowing herself as a seed in the earth, taking herself into the fist and throwing herself away, closing her nose tight and hiding in a stream. She says that she feels like pouring lead into her ears unable to hear her being called 'reservation category', the same punishment that the caste system had reserved for Dalits for listening to the Vedas! She expresses the desire to bury herself, shed herself, kill herself, escape and punish herself. She is conscious of her identity as well as the consequences of her being recognized as a Dalit woman by society. Is she trying to distance herself from the self as viewed by the society or is she is trying to get rid of her identity? Her wish to lose herself movingly portrays the frustration of people who are discriminated, exploited and ill-treated as they develop contempt for their identity. The identity that emerges here is that of a Dalit woman who is viewed as a thing by the 'other' and who longs to eliminate herself.

The poem presents Dalit women of different ages, who are in different professions or stages. It could even be the journey of the same Dalit woman. She becomes the field labourer whose modesty is also exploited like her toil is. She becomes the Dalit girl who steps into the hostel building for education after crossing several obstacles. She turns into a Dalit Christian girl who is abused in school as a *bindiless* (without a dot, that is bindi, on forehead) and later as a casteless girl. As a woman her identity is ridiculed when she learns that as a Dalit woman she can only satisfy lust but cannot be the wife of an upper caste man who plays with her in the name of love. Ultimately her struggle is rewarded. She becomes part of the state machinery. But, she cannot escape the murmurs about her reserved category. That is the last straw on the camel's back. She decides to bloom like the flame of the forest and leap like the stream across the forests of hardships. She evolves from a Dalit woman who was only an object of exploitation earlier into a Dalit woman who is ready to revolt. It is her experiences and struggle that teach her to revolt. The image of washing her life in the flames of suffering and blooming like a *mankena* (a red coloured) flower reminds one of Sita's fire ordeal thus reiterating the casteist belief of fire as the purifier. This image reminding us of an upper caste/class stereotype proves how Dalit women writers also use and subvert the stereotypical images.

Apart from raising the issue of the identity politics of the community, this discussion raises the issue of personal identity. It establishes an identity that is moulded against the stereotypes, apprehensions, assumptions and judgements about Dalit women by the other, whether it is society in general or upper caste men, upper caste women, Dalit men as separate categories, who are relatively speaking, in a superior or decisive position. This includes an evaluation of their situation, ideology and writings. Dalit women's narratives make an effort to say that what others have been saying about them is wrong. They try to condemn this misinterpretation or misrepresentation by the upper caste society or the Dalit society itself. For instance, the editor's words in *Nallapoddu* deconstruct the Dalit men's notion of Dalit women as well. While locating Dalit women and Dalit women's writing, the editor of *Nallapoddu* makes thought-provoking observations. Here I have specifically chosen the discussion under the head 'Dalit Movements and Women's Questions' since it raises the curtain over a crucial debate on the gender question in caste movements. The editor says that though Dalit writers have made pathbreaking contributions to Telugu literature, they have illustrated patriarchal tendencies towards Dalit women. They express certain views which demean the self-respect of Dalit women. She comes up with the agenda that compensation and self-respect have to become equally important in Dalit struggle against atrocities on Dalit women. She hits back at the male Dalit writers who demeaningly proclaim that using abusive language is Dalit culture. She expresses the fear that gradually culture of exploitation may continue as culture of the victimized. It is in fact the mimicking of Hindu culture which influences Dalit men. Dalit men have not recognized Dalit woman as a being with rights and a force to contend with but look at her only as a victim who stands in the shelter of Dalit men: 'The tradition of looking at Dalit men while talking about Dalits and at dominant caste women while talking about women is being continued in the theorization of Dalit movement.'[7] This reminds one of bell hooks' effort to theorize the status of Black women in Black and Feminist movements. This debate on identity politics which is seen across marginalized literatures where either the woman of the exploited sections is appropriated by the feminist movement thus alienating her from 'her people's struggle' or the race or caste movements categorically declaring that their women have no gender problems and they need liberation not from their men but from racial discrimination. Bell Hooks says,

Racist, sexist socialization had conditioned us to devalue our femaleness and to regard race as the only relevant label of identification. In other words, we were asked to deny a part of ourselves . . . and we did . . . we were afraid to acknowledge that sexism could be just as oppressive as racism . . . we were a new generation of black women who had been taught to submit, to accept sexual inferiority and to be silent.[8]

This is the process of negotiating one's identity especially in a situation where one is attributed multiple identities, and when all these identities are political and are debated by themselves as well as the other.

It also reminds one of Vimal Thorat's anguish and concern that Dalit woman is being victimized by Dalit men as well. The fear of Dalit men of Dalit women that she speaks of reiterates the competence and the calibre of Dalit women. Thorat explains how both the Dalit movement and the women's movement have consciously ignored the Dalit women's issue. She also attacks Bahujan Samaj Party for sidelining or handling the issues concerning Dalit women extremely peripherally while it is articulate about the caste identity. She questions,

We have now two generations of articulate, committed Dalit women professionals who are lecturers, professors, activists. But their articulation threatens the Dalit male leadership. They will find no place on their committees! Their presence itself will be a threat to their articulations that refuse to articulate the issue of brutal violence against Dalit women, gender violence and nuts and bolts issues like

69

the right to water and a life of dignity. Forty years after the Dalit movement, where is the women's share?[9]

All these arguments that create constant binaries of different categories make the identity politics much more specific and focused simultaneously strengthening the larger identity politics and movements.

While Dalit men writers discuss the discrimination meted out to them and question the deception and desertion that they have faced from upper caste men, Dalit women writers question upper caste women and specifically feminists as to when Dalit women were part of the feminist movement. Especially, a powerful Dalit woman's voice like that of Challapalli Swarooparani repeatedly comments about feminist movement where there is no place for lower caste and lower class women and poses questions about the upper caste feminism which confines itself to the constricting kitchens but does not extend to the kitchenless houses of the downtrodden:

> Oh my blue cloud that taught us to rain!
> The showers of your questions
> came only till all-equipped kitchen
> why didn't they even step on the threshold
> of my homeless three-stoned stove?[10]

Thus, while trying to establish solidarity, trying to identify themselves with certain issues, sympathize and empathize with other suffering sections, Dalit women also establish their identities very clearly so as to present their argument powerfully.

Similar to this, Jajula Gowri's introduction to 'Naa Payanam (My Journey)' starts with 'born, brought up in mud, ate mud and wrote mud writings. I am a mud being. I am a mere mud being'.[11] While this starting gives a crucial cue to her portrayal of self, her writings portray people from lower class and lower caste background who are born and brought up in mud but reach heights of achievement with hard work and perseverance. Obviously, the few words that she uses to describe herself do not talk about her caste except a hint at her class and professional background of her family unless we connect class and caste. It is only after reading her introduction that we understand how her caste background associates her with her ideological leanings.

Let us look at her use of words in her poem 'As I Am'[12] for describing Dalits, Madigas specifically. 'Making a Panchama', 'pushing to the outskirts', 'destroy', 'thrust the profession', 'bonded labour', 'grinding me to flour'—all these suggest victimization of Madigas. Reference to 'my Panchama brother' makes her location much more specific. The flesh is eaten away and blood oozes out, what remains is only bones. Their own brothers are ready to grind even the bones to flour. The hierarchy of caste system sees to it that the lowest section of the society is victimized by all the above sections. Her describing the unity mantra as a hollow one leading to pain and suffering throws light on the futility of arguing for unity of categorization among Dalits and the burden it thrusts on Madigas. This is like professing unity among non-Dalits and Dalits. How can there be unity when there is discrimination combined with hierarchy?

She describes 'human beings with no humanness' and expresses the desire to get separated from them. It is her longing to find her place and protect herself as she is. She is tired of being sandwiched between yesterday, today and tomorrow. When she says that she wants to project herself as she is, what is 'she' as she is? Is she talking about herself or her Madiga community? When she states her decision to fight, is she not constructing the Madiga Porata Samithi from the eyes of a Madiga? What is most important about the poem 'As I Am' is that apart from talking about her community, caste-conflict, political movements, she overtly expresses her political stance, thus throwing light on the political dimension of her identity.

This also leads us to the question of the nation as narrated by Dalit writers. Early writers like Gurram Jashuva, Jala Rangaswamy, Kusuma Dharmanna, Tadi Nagamma and others express their loyalties to their community as well as to the country and strive for the liberation of both. While Tadi Nagamma's short story 'Oka Muddu' projects the protagonist, a young woman, as a courageous and persevering freedom fighter, Kusuma Dharmanna's *Makoddi Nalladoratanam* (We Don't Want the Black Bossism strikes back at the white colonialism as well as the local caste hierarchy. He poses questions to society:

> Didn't our parents give birth to us?
> like your parents did to you?
> Is not birth same to you and to us?
> Are not the blood and flesh same?
> Do you only have pain and pleasure and not us?
> Is it not the same God to you and to us?
> Is it not the same religion to you and to us?
> Why this argument and difference, is it fair of you?[13]

Like his contemporaries, Kusuma Dharmanna also reiterates the claim of Dalits to Hinduism. It is not the negation of Hinduism that we see in these writings, but an appeal to the dominant castes to accept their right over Hinduism. They attempt to reform their community as well as the discriminating Hinduism. It is here that the most crucial religious identities of Dalits emerge. Still, Dalits were mostly being referred to either by their caste names or as untouchables or as Harijans. Although Ambedkar was the guiding star, Gandhi had his inspiring hold on 'untouchables'. It was still reformation that Dalits were talking about, not alteration.

While some of these speakers establish themselves as potential role models and successful warriors, some of the speakers tend to empathize with the suffering of Dalit women, thus establishing solidarity and identification. While it is true that Dalit women writers quite often use 'I' as 'we' or shift between 'I' and 'we', it is not that they try to project the Dalit woman as a homogeneous category. They are aware of the differences and divisions based on various criteria. That is why we come across a range of characters and issues in Dalit women's writing, representing the variety of life. The oral narratives included in this project also represent a similar consciousness of the differences and different identities. Although they do not overtly speak about the differences among Dalits and their political implications, they do express the uniqueness of different identities.

Religious identities play an important role in the political stand that the writers take. While written texts have expressed great awareness of this religious hierarchy and have attempted to subvert the same, oral narratives, except those of the activists, express unawareness of this debate or just ignore this issue and the narrators identify themselves as Hindus or Christians. One of the women who is interviewed for this project, who is an MPTC member, speaks as a Hindu SC. Her Hindu identity that she wants to protect and preserve but is not allowed to do so is what emerges from her experiences of not being allowed into temples, even on festival days, and being driven away as an 'untouchable' though she does not use the word 'untouchable'. Does she speak for the Hindu-Dalit situation where Dalits are not even allowed near the threshold of the temple? Like they are 'helped' at the water sources by 'generous and kind' non-Dalits, Dalits are 'mediated' at the temples. While the offerings of Dalits are accepted, they are not accepted and admitted. She may not know about the temple entry movements for Dalits. But, she speaks as one whose people are always kept away and outside. At the same time, like most Dalits, she convinces herself that at least her offerings are accepted. She is aware of the fact that she is invited to the temple only because of her political status. It is not that the villagers have forgotten the caste difference or her untouchability. Hence, her reluctance to step into the temple. Here is a case of a woman who is capable, intelligent and efficient but is forced to remain passive and silent. It could also be interpreted as acceptance that emerges from helplessness.

This acceptance in most cases is seen because of the necessity of livelihood. For instance, one Chindu woman accepts begging as her profession and her dependence on Madigas, on whom Chindu people are traditionally dependent. Moreover, she raises questions like, how will she survive if she does not beg and who will give her food if she does not plead for it. These questions reveal the institutional conditioning of people who conform to the norms that are inflicted on them in the name of tradition. On the other hand, how else will she survive in a system which has allotted her the traditional profession? A landless, property-less lone woman with nobody to look after her in her old age—what is the role of a welfare state? Her questions interrogate and find fault with the state as well.

In fact, any discussion of folk art forms will inevitably bring to mind people like Gaddar, Guda Anjaiah, Masterji, Gorati Venkanna and others who have greatly contributed to Telugu Dalit literature with their songs. Song is one of the major forms of any oral literature. While Dalit literature asserts that song is part of Dalit literature and borrows generously from it quite often, some of the above outstanding personalities have become living legends using traditional art forms in the contemporary context thus taking back song to common people once again. If we raise the question, is it not flourishing of traditional art, it remains a question because any attempt to answer this will bring in many more embarrassing questions.

Also, another Chindu woman raises a few very crucial questions about folk art forms. They no longer can provide sustenance to people. There could be several reasons for that.

Changing tastes of people, migration from villages to cities, changing lifestyles, so on and so forth. It is also true that art forms like Chindu Bhagotham are confined to a particular caste which is a dependent caste on Madigas. It puts them on the lowest strata of society which is at the mercy of the other remaining castes of society. While we are talking about the preservation of folk art forms, do we take into consideration the dependence that it creates for lower castes on the privileged sections and the issues of survival of the performing people? Is it justified to ask these sections to preserve these art forms in spite of starvation and hardships while the rest of the society accesses technology and progress? While any art form aims to appease the intellectual and aesthetic requirements of the audience, it comes into existence basically as a survival strategy of the artists, in most cases especially the folk forms. Hence, the importance of the Chindu woman's statement about Chindu Bhagotham—hunger and begging. They have become beggars from artists. But, according to the dominant sections of the society they have always been 'untouchables'.

It is the acceptance of this tradition that makes Lachhavva, Dakkali Lachhi say that it is their right to beg from Madigas and it is the responsibility of Madigas to give. She accepts the untouchability meted out to them by Madigas on whom they are dependent by tradition. This is the identity of herself that she constructs proudly as an untouchable dependent on Madiga community. What is surprising is the absolute acceptance and no-complaint attitude in her tone. Like Chindu people accepting their performance of folk arts and begging, Dakkalis accept their predicament of begging. This is what the tradition has taught them. One is tempted to examine this in the light of the Dalit movement and the protest against suppressive and oppressive traditions. Not all Dalits are aware of the reform or revolt movements but change has crept into some castes of Dalit sections alone. Most of these dependent castes still are not even touched by change and have not even resented the internal hierarchies. When and how will they be part of larger movements like the Dalit movement or a political revolution like the Bahujan Samaj Party?

Also, different generations contribute to particular identities and ideologies. One 'Mala' woman compares past with present. While comparing these two, she constructs her life as well as her identity. 'They' are Malas. They are different from Madigas. Her identity is the identity of her community. She talks about herself, her family, her community, her village. She has witnessed deaths in her life. Her family is broken and divided. She looks at herself as a woman whose family has witnessed several losses and deaths but has to survive and exist as the crucial pole of the family. Yet, she has not lost hope in life. She still talks about her land with no bore wells and no water like a typical farmer. Her goal, her destination is survival with no big hopes in life.

Her caste does not trouble her, does not subject her to humiliation. But, on the other hand, she throws light on the living together feature of her village. Malas and Madigas live together in that village; while generally they live in two different streets away from the village, away from each other since Malas also practice caste hierarchy towards Madigas. She does not know anything about political development like Madiga struggle against Mala hierarchy and the movement for the categorization of reservations. But, she mirrors the difference between these two castes and reiterates the hierarchy. While she does not refer to the upper caste hegemony against them, she asserts their superiority over Madigas.

Dalit women writers assert their identity as Dalit women and at the same time they express the sense of alienation and exile in their society. According to them, they have contributed to the glorious history of this country but they have no place here for they are untouchables. They belong to the country that has subjected Dalit women to the double-edged weapon of discrimination and exploitation based on caste and gender. The labels that the society has imposed on them haunt and hound them towards the outskirts. Vinodini, in her poem 'A Single Pole Hut' says,

> This caste became a huge Lucifer
> turned me who had strayed
> into a Christian lamb by his touch
> and left me in the outskirts.[14]

This reiterates the binary of you and we that marks Dalit women's narratives. Upper caste society looks at Dalits as uncivilized and polluting. It is not the Dalits polluting the upper caste people, but as M. Gowri says in her poem,

> Conscience-killed human corpses are not here
> May be available in your bedrooms.
> There are human beings with flesh and blood here
> Human beings full of life are here. [Translation mine][15]

The poem throws a challenge to the upper caste man by establishing a binary of lower caste woman and upper caste man. It tries to establish certain qualities of these two sections. While Dalit community is characterized by courage and adventure, upper caste society is characterized by cowardice. The emphasis of Dalit literature on 'life' is reiterated here. Dalits are full of life, nature is a close associate of Dalits, their eating of animals is not violence, but making the maximum out of animals, thus revealing their close association with nature. The poet not only sings the glory of her community but also puts herself in the position of a teacher to a 'traditional teacher'. She can teach him how to collect bones and will show him the unbent spinal cord. His fingers shedding the dirt and becoming a mridangam (a percussion instrument) after cleaning the hide is probably the ultimate subversion of the concepts of purity, untouchability and pollution. The poem is a challenge to the so-called non-violent communities by the lower caste, Dalit 'violent' cultures. It also establishes the beauty of the working class toil and courage.

This new being that has emerged never forgets her past because her desire and effort to change herself and change the society have their roots in the oppressive past. On one hand, the writer presents the past and on the other the present and future. Shyamala rightly says, 'Oppression is my past, revolt is my present and future'[16] in her poem 'I am a Varadagudu'. While these women are talking about self, past and future, no doubt they are talking about women like themselves whose lives have gone astray due to the stigma attached to their community identity. These are also writers who speak about the personal life, failures mostly and their reactions. It is the personal life but moulded by the larger politics of caste and gender.

Dalit women have been choosing their models very carefully. Although initially Gandhi inspired Dalit communities with his reformist ideology, Dalit communities have always had their own models and in contemporary times they are choosing their models much more politically. Dalit women like Sadalakshmi, Chandrasri, Phulan Devi, Alisamma and others who fought against the casteist and patriarchal structures of the society and who contributed to the rebuilding of the social structures and who redefined the cultural constraints are the role models for Dalit women writers. Gogu Shyamala states who are her role models and why:

My mother is Muthamma, younger sister Phulan Devi
oppression is my past, revolt is my present and future
my target caste, my victory Durban.

Not only her role models but her destinations and ideologies are also very clear. In fact the models that she has chosen give her the discretion to choose her path and the determination to reach the goals.

In all this, the loyalties of Dalit women to the country are declared without any hesitation. What they are concerned about is how to make their position much more secure in society. One more important thing that these accounts remind us of is the scholarship or the writing skills of these writers, thus also projecting their identities as writers and scholars. In contrast to this, Vinodini establishes her identity as 'a suspected outsider' in Hindu society as a Dalit Christian. Discussing the specific context of Graham Stein's brutal murder, the poem articulates the fear and insecurity of minorities. Her location as a Dalit Christian in a village setup in 'A Single Pole Hut' shifts to the larger situation of India where minorities are made to live on a razor's edge escaping from the haunting tridents and frightening saffron. Although she is talking in the first person narrative, she gives voice to the anxieties of millions of minorities. What she has lost is the coin of faith without which one's survival becomes a burden.

Her identity of a minority gets firmly established with her extensive use of Christian analogy as she does in her other writings as well. This establishes her identity as a person who is thoroughly into a religion intellectually, emotionally, socially and culturally. Same is the case with Vijayabharathi who reveals her knowledge of Hinduism quite often in her writings by criticizing it thoroughly. Thus, religious identities become political identities as religious identities are used for political purposes by the State and the people. She questions,

To respectably insult the upper caste women and meanly and harshly insult the lower caste and labour class people is the culture of the Puranas. Taking racial and other kinds of revenge on women is seen in literature as well as in history. . . . Chastity—common people cannot understand the culture of declaring on one hand that *pativratya* is most important to women and trying to spoil that *pativratya* on the other hand. What is the intention of Vishnu (in disguise) spoiling the chastity of Jalandhara's wife, Tulasi? Is it because she is a Dalit woman?[17]

Her writings are rooted in her location as a Dalit woman and they offer the relevant tools to understand the duplicity involved in the Puranas that have been functioning as texts of instructions for society in the name of religion and spirituality.

A similar thing happens in other narratives as well whether it is in the case of Dalit women politicians who hesitate to step into the temple, or Chindu women who surrender to the tradition or the Mala woman who reiterates her caste superiority. While Christian women, in their writings, seem to stress on their changed identities thus reflecting on their urge to escape from the suffocating caste system and ultimately being labelled as Dalit Christians, the oral narratives try to establish a religious identity which is ruled more by tradition, lacking revolt either at a personal or a community level.

The oral and written narratives discussed in this project help us to understand the multiple identities that the term Dalit woman carries with it. These multiple identities are not different layers like watertight compartments—clearly bifurcated and strictly defined. Some of them may even be overlapping. The differences of subcaste, class, occupation, region, social status and achievements give 'the Dalit woman' the unique individuality and eventually lead to the culmination in the form of a Dalit woman's consciousness. With all these differences society looks at them and treats them as outsiders and the same status and treatment motivate Dalit women towards solidarity in order to resolve their conflicts and fight battles together against 'the other'.

NOTES

1. Mary Madiga, published in *Nallapoddu: Dalit Strila Sahityam 1921–2002*, Hyderabad: Hyderabad Book Trust, 2002, pp. 370–1.
2. Dakkali Lachhavva collected by Narayana, *Chupu,* January–April 1997, pp. 4–5.
3. Anupama Rao, *The Caste Question: Dalits and the Politics of Modern India*, Ranikhet: Permanent Black, 2010, p. 89.
4. Nagappagari Sundarraju, *Madigodu: Nagappagari Sundarraju Kathalu*, Hyderabad: Madiga Sahitya Vedika, 1997.
5. Gogu Shyamala, 'The Wound' from Flowering from the Soil: Dalit Women's Writing from Telugu, pp. 239–55.
6. Published in G. Lakshminarasaiah, ed., *Padunekkina Paata: Dalita Kavitvam*, Vijayawada: Dalita Sana Prachuranalu, 1996, pp. 3–4.
7. Gogu Shyamala, *Nallapoddu*, p. 25.
8. Bell Hooks, *Ain't I a Woman: Black Woman and Feminism*, Boston MA: South End Press, 1981, pp. 1–2.
9. Vimal Thorat, p. 8.
10. Challapalli Swarooparani, *Mankenapoovu*, pp. 149–50.
11. Jajula Gowri, *Mannubuvva: Kathalu*, Hyderabad: Samajika Tatvika Viswavidyalayam, 2004.
12. Jajula Gowri, 'As I Am', *Madiga Chaitanyam: Madiga Kavula Sankalanam*, Hyderabad: Madiga Sahitya Vedika, p. 24.
13. Kusuma Dharmanna, *Maakoddi Nalladoratanam*, Hyderabad: Hyderabad Book Trust, 2003, p. 21.
14. M.M.Vinodini,'A Single Pole Hut', tr. K. Suneetha Rani, *Chandrabhaga*, no. 2, 2000, pp. 3–5.
15. M. Gowri,'The Ripe Hands', in *Madiga Chaithanyam: Madiga Kavula Sankalanam*, ed. Nagappagari Sundarraju, Hyderabad: Madiga Sahitya Vedika, 1997, pp. 15–16.
16. Gogu Shyamala, 'I am a Varadagoodu', in *Flowering from the Soil: Dalit Women's Writing from Telugu*, p. 230.
17. Vijayabharathi, *Nallapoddu*, p. 128.

6

Rural and Urban

OST OF THE women interviewed for this project are either rooted in villages or connected to villages in one way or the other. Village in their narratives becomes not only a geographical entity but an agency that shapes the lives of the Dalit women. Whenever there is a reference to the village, there is also a reference to the urban in the narratives. However, the rural and the urban are always juxtaposed as oppositional binaries.

In one of the narratives, the description of the village is so vivid that the boundaries and the restrictions of the village come alive. The narrator not only emphasizes that the conditions are bad in her village but also wishes that the conditions become better. According to her, everything should be equal and that equality will give a good future to her children. She admits that caste exists in the village. 'If we go near them, they say don't touch us. Here, it is definitely there. It may not be much in the cities. But, it is there in these villages.' Such a description also subverts the nostalgia and longing that is established for the rural in a country like India. A village does not merely stand for the plenty and the green but it also stands for a clearly drawn picture of discrimination and difference. The lines are so rigidly drawn that they can never be erased. What is said in a very positive manner about the Indian rural life that everyone knows about everyone can be read in practical terms as everyone knows about everyone's caste in any Indian village.

The invincible casteist hierarchical structures press down the people, especially women and lower castes in a village. The oppressed people hopefully look at the visible and the invisible. Some such people find a solution in urban areas. For one of the Dalit women interviewed, town life stands for education and equality. She describes how her daughter studying in a town is part of the egalitarian practices that her friends are following. Her daughter studies in a private English medium school and stays in a hostel. She says that girls of all castes move together like sisters and eat food from one plate. According to her, it is a kind of liberation and town is a site of equality.

The urban, in contrast to the rural here assumes a major role as a borderless, no-bias, ideal place. Apart from that, the urban space can accommodate an English medium school and a hostel that unites girls hailing from different backgrounds. The absence of a typical, fraternal identification of people by name and community in an urban situation contributes to the erasure of 'untouchable' identity seems to be the understanding of the narrator.

Similarly, another narrative also traces the picture of the village by saying that there are problems in the village but there are elders and the cadre of the party to resolve them. Her meaningful pause after 'I am also an elder, but ...' speaks volumes about her inability to do anything for the village or for herself.

She does not specifically mention whether it is the party or the village that pressurized her to contest in the elections.

Either way she wants to convey that it was not her choice to contest the elections, but theirs. It is not that she was forced to contest the elections but that she was acceptable to all of them. She appears to be moving between having an agency and not having an agency as a Dalit woman. That she is able to speak out on the conditions in which she contested the elections, how she is made to remain passive and she is not able to do anything for the village and herself reveals her agency and brings out the questioning woman in her.

She also subtly reveals how they have no steady and assured work in the village but have to keep looking around for work. On the other hand, it is the same village that elevated her to the level of a people's representative. It gave her the space and the opportunity to move from a wage labourer to a political leader. Although she was 'chosen' by the village or the political party, she tries to say that she deserved that choice. Even when she almost complains that she does not go for the meetings as her husband does not trust her to go there unaccompanied by him, she tries to excuse him by saying that the journey is difficult—in a village like hers with only three buses a day and that too at odd times.

A similar story comes out in another narrative when the narrator repeatedly refers to her village. Like the speaker referred to previously, she is a labourer. She begins her narrative by speaking of what the village thought about her. According to her, the village thought that she was an innocent one and will definitely win the elections if she contests. One wonders why she is defending herself—not only on her own behalf but also on behalf of the village.

She says again that she cannot lie and cheat, once again emphasizing her 'innocence' as the accused. She continues to say that all villagers, including 'her people' wondered how a labourer woman would get into elections. The contradiction in her narrative about the village and the villagers and the clarification about her innocence can be traced to the hurdles and conspiracies that she faced as a people's representative who was not allowed to take up any work and who landed up in a trap of debts. She also mentions that she won over three villages to assert her victory against the image of an innocent labourer woman whose victory is suspect. In order to assert her victory against the image of an innocent labourer woman, whose very victory is suspect, she mentions that she won over not just one but three villages.

A schoolteacher who is brought up in a town and who works in a village brings up very interesting insights when she discusses her understanding of the dynamics of a village. She asserts that casteism exists in villages. Her living space and her workplace are positioned in a contradictory manner as the earlier one is associated with her friends, social circle, acceptability while the latter is associated with labelling, alienation and discrimination.

She rightly points out that most villagers migrate to other places. All children belonging to the affording, privileged castes go to private schools, join the expensive hostels and move to the urban space. It is only the lower caste and lower class children who attend the government schools in villages. For her, school represents the village as her interaction with the village is also through the school.

She also tries to intervene in the dialogue between the children. She says that SC children in villages are angry with upper caste children. But, she tries to pacify them by saying that they cannot achieve anything by being angry. Getting educated is the only as, for instance, they respect her, in spite of knowing her caste identity, only because of her education.

On the other hand, she says that there is no casteism among teachers. Is it the community, the education or the status as a teacher that contributes to their non-casteist tendencies? Once again, she juxtaposes the teachers coming from the urban and representing the urban against the village where people respect her as long as they do not know her identity but stop doing so once they come to know about it. In her narrative, the village has a caste and casteism but the teachers do not. Their community identities are not revealed anywhere.

Similarly, she refers to her brahmin friends who eat at her place. Is she interpreting this as the impact of education and urban space? According to her, children learn the caste details and caste language from their parents. Again, she brings together the two spaces—home and school to build the impact on the children in terms of caste. It is the urban space that she seems to believe as the liberating space while the village still believes and behaves with a casteist agenda.

In case of the narrator who is branded as a witch, the village plays the role of a punishing agency. There is the case of a woman who was married to an older man and got into a relationship with another married man. She justifies her action by saying that she wanted children which the older man was not capable of giving her. The younger man is from another village and so both the villages come into the picture with all their controlling and conditioning forces.

The man and the woman belonging to two different villages along with the boy born to them, take shelter in the temple when the boy falls ill. The temple that they believe would be the place of blessing and healing turns out to be a site of violence when the villagers enter the temple and beat up the couple. In fact, temple represents the ultimate power and hegemony that a village can hold. The man and the woman could transgress the boundaries of home and village but they could not transgress the restrictions of the two villages that were playing the role of the moral police.

They reached the temple travelling from homes through their villages. The temple does not solve the problem of her son's ill-health but poses more problems by using violence against them and invoking the norms of morality and conduct and marital traditions. That is when the woman approached the court with a hope that at least the judiciary will resolve the problem.

It is the sarpanch (elected head of a village-level statutory institution of local self-government called the panchayat) and the patwari (a government official who keeps records regarding the ownership of land) who represent the village but not all villagers together. She is pulled up for not having taken permission from the sarpanch and the patwari. She says that she asked them if she has to take permission from the sarpanch to go to God. These questions could also be about their caste status though the narrator seems to be saying that she was being penalized for having an extra-marital relationship. The beating that she received could also be due to their 'untouchable' identity. The village that the Dalit women discuss needs to be mentioned at various levels—geographical, cultural, political and social.

Another narrative presents a vivid description of the village by explaining how communities are located in the village. Her childhood village was crowded whereas now it is not crowded due to migration, not only from the village to elsewhere but also from within the village. Her village is characterized by mobility in the location of the communities. Malas and Madigas do not any longer live in the space that the village has specified for them. Colonies constructed by the government have encouraged them to move from there and relocate themselves, though not to become a part of the mainstream but to live in the outskirts, once again.

Her concern for migration stands for the concern of a generation which has a very strong attachment with the place it belongs to. It cannot really be compared to dislocation and displacement in a larger sense, because it is the pucca houses that the government got constructed as part of better facilities for

Dalits that take Dalits away from their original habitation. It is not force but hope that drives them. But, for the above narrator, it caused disturbance in her village which was crowded with houses and people. She also expresses concern that nowadays people do not follow differences. As one for traditions, she is alarmed by this. At the same time, she establishes the religious identity of her community as one that does not go to 'any temples' but worships and conducts rituals for Yellamma, their traditional Goddess. While she says no to 'Hindu' gods, goddesses and rituals, she reiterates the hierarchy constructed by Hinduism. This sense of community life or community identity moulds Dalit women's writing as well.

Descriptions of the village do not end here but extend into the phase of migration from one village to another village or towards a town. Even if it is forced migration, in some cases it brings a change in the life and self-image of people, like for instance, the story of a young girl who went to the town as a domestic help. Her primary schooling was stopped to send her as a domestic to the city. She says that the migration, even though it was child labour and dislocation, helped her in educating herself and boosted her wish and determination to get educated.

To go back to the schoolteacher, she presents two situations, one rural and the second semi-urban. She tries to say that in spite of her identity, she was not discriminated against in a semi-urban situation. But the comments of her friends do sarcastically refer to her caste. In the rural situation, as long as her identity is not revealed, her situation is secure. Her position changes once it is revealed. Her students' reaction to her caste throws light on the general discourse of caste differences and how they enter into every field of life. What she does not speak about here is her religious identity. While it is obvious that she is not a Christian, her Hindu identity might have got her some initial acceptance into certain circles. This has to be studied in the context of Dalit women writers saying that caste and religion have become two major haunting forces which they cannot shed in spite of trying hard to do so.

It is a fact Dalit women's situation adds to the caste-class-gender identity of Dalit women. For instance, the above narrator is a woman who has moved from semi-urban situation to rural situation. She constructs herself in different contexts. She says that she has not experienced discrimination when she was a student or now as a working woman. Although initially she 'refuses' to accept the fact that she is insulted and ridiculed, the examples that she gives prove the contrary. She contradicts herself. She knows what her identity is according to the society. But, her self-esteem refuses to admit her vulnerable position. Although she does not make a statement, her experiences that she narrates speak volumes about her identity crisis and the dilemma between her reality and her self-esteem. One other narrator also reiterates that caste system or caste discrimination, to be specific, does exist in rural areas, thus not only exposing the system but also identifying herself as a rural person. While doing so, she creates an imaginary binary by speaking from her assumption or hope that probably discrimination may be relatively less in urban areas.

A similar concern for increasing migration is also seen in Gujjarlamudi Nirmalarani's article.[1] Locating herself against rural background in a famine-stricken district, Nirmalarani analyses social, political, cultural and economic issues related to or resulting from famine. The instances of migration that she cites are caused by famine, strained human relations, debt-webs, etc. This reminds one of the woman sarpanch who was supposed to and was entitled to implement the food for work scheme in order to prevent migration—she herself was forced to migrate in search of livelihood.

Nirmalarani brilliantly connects the state policies, famine situation, consumer culture, hopes for easy money, evil social practices, domestic violence and women's predicament.

Although she does not talk about herself, her essay reveals her as an informed, conscientious, committed and thoughtful activist. Her use of various factors like caste, class, region and profession in order to present a thought-provoking perspective of the contemporary situation shows her as the one who is knowledgeable about the contemporary situation. She does present specific identities related to the above mentioned categories. At the same time, her concentration is on gender. When she is arguing about the influence of larger issues on women's lives, her consciousness of and concern for a drought-stricken, poverty-ridden region almost touches the region-specific writings that were/are being produced in regions like Telangana and Rayalaseema. Similar themes get extended to her fiction as well. For instance, her short story 'Gaju Kallu' (Lifeless Eyes) depicts the struggle of a family for livelihood and how, unable to cultivate their land due to influencing factors in the region, the women get into sex work. Added to this is the question of rural life that she seems to emphasize repeatedly. She tries to say, like the Dalit women's narratives, how villages were earlier different from urban areas but how the greedy and evil practices have not spared even rural areas now. On the other hand, the urban areas have also become equally divided by casteism like the rural areas.

NOTE

1. Published in *Maanavi*, April 2004, Hyderabad, pp. 30–4.

7

Childhood and Education

REPRESENTATION OF childhood in Dalit narratives dismantles the glorious childhood that is constructed and longed for in nostalgia by the privileged mainstream. In Dalit narratives, childhood is one of hunger, poverty, suffering, responsibilities and struggle. However, at the same time, it does not mean that the Dalit childhood is only a gloomy picture. It may not be a romanticized and idealized childhood but it has got its own wishes and joys and its own expressions marked by goals and aspirations.

The narratives that are recorded for this project also have similar representations of childhood, which are a combination of hard work, restrictions, subversions and small achievements. Interestingly, all the narratives have reference to childhood in one way or the other. Some women talked about their childhood while others talked about their children's childhood. In most cases, there is a juxtaposition of 'my childhood' and 'my children's childhood'. This also functioned as markers of change for them in terms of caste differences and cultural transformations.

Village in their childhood was more casteist and in their children's childhood it is being left behind by them to access education and improve their lives. Childhood also pushed some of them into oppressive practices and traditions from which they could never get out.

In all these representations, there is an integral reference to education. Either they say that they are not educated or that they are educating their children or that they wish they had studied. They attribute the reasons for the discrimination that they suffer to lack of education and wish that education will rescue their children from all patterns of subjugation. Hence, this chapter has chosen to discuss childhood and education in these narratives. These two cannot be discussed separately in the context of these narratives. It examines how education becomes the centre of the narrator's' concern for development and esteem.

The *jogini* woman says that she was given to the temple when she was very young. Her childhood came to an end at seven when she was made a *jogini*. Her brother was sent to school while she was given to the temple. While he went on to get a job and have a family of his own, she had to beg as a *jogini* in the village. She later lost even that livelihood when government banned *jogini* system and was at the same time disowned by her family. Her life shows how the incidents in her childhood paved way for her painful future and how her predicament was decided by her family, community and society in her early years itself.

She looks back at her childhood as a decisive point in her life and compares herself with her friends who continued schooling while she could not do so. For her, childhood is integrated with education. It is her deprivation of education that made her not say anything against the decision to give her as a *jogini*. Her uninformed childhood was also another reason, she says. She did not know what she was doing and she could not protest as she was very young. What we hear in her narrative about her childhood is not a nostalgic recalling of the glorious time but a lament that her childhood did not know what was happening to her. 'If I were to know in childhood, I would have gone to a house (married). But, they made me like this when I didn't know anything in childhood. If I were to know, I would not have been in this.' She thinks she could have reverted the situation if only she had education and a source of survival.

Gogu Shyamala in an interview says,

Education is always a must and essential for Dalits. My education was like a battle. I had to fight for it, in fact. Since, though I am a girl, my parents gave my education greater importance than that was given to my brothers. So, my brothers had to work hard so as to earn the money and spend the same on my education. It was only with the help of my entire family including my brothers that I had completed my intermediate studies withstanding all hardship. Including lot of hurdles and immense societal pressure, that was all there, pestering and forcing my father to give up sending me to college studies only for the reason that we are Dalits.[1]

Education has been a battle for most of the women interviewed for this project, whether it is their own education or their children's. However, not all of them got support from the family like Gogu Shyamala mentions she got from her family.

A young shepherdess reveals an effort to come out of the complex situation that she is entangled in. Her destination is clear and her complaints are against her father. Her gender identity which is responsible for her being deprived of education, surfaces here; though her social and economic status also contributes to her childhood being spent among the cattle. She creates an image of her own as a child forced to get into hard toil and pulled out from school. This in fact breaks the glorified and romantic depiction of the image of a Dalit girl among cattle. Like any other child, she too does not enjoy menial work and spending valuable years of her personality-formation in the fields. Like any other child she too gets suffocated and burdened, feels like revolting against her father but cannot and comes to terms with her predicament. There is a feature of self-respect and dignity that characterizes this life-struggle. She raises crucial questions about childhood, gender, labour, class and caste. Her anger with her parents, especially her father, is because she is not sent to school. She does not have great ambitions and destination, but her only dream is to go to school. What that education gives her, she is not sure about. As her father says, it may not guarantee her a job. However, all these words of discouragement do not disappoint her but increase the determination in her to go to school. Her dreams of standing on her own feet, according to her, can only be fulfilled by getting educated. Not that she does not understand her position. But the gender bias in the family angers her and insults her. She presents herself as a girl child who is subjected to gender discrimination at home and to insults, ridicules and teasing outside. But, she does not lose hope.

Four siblings, all girls, are not sent to school but the younger brother is sent to school. The narrator, who is one of the four girl children, wants to study at least to read the bus boards and she strongly believes that one can stand on one's feet only with the help of education. She says, 'If we ask him to send us to school he says what do you get by going to school, how will you become better? What will you do if we send you to school, if it is your brother, he will look after us.' She is sent for grazing the sheep as she repeatedly asks her father about her schooling. Father declares that though she is grazing the sheep, they will be given to her brother but will not be distributed among the sisters.

On the other hand, her mother, like other Dalit women in these narratives, wants to educate her daughters. But, the reason for this is not her vision for her daughter's development like it is in the case of other narratives. She thinks that her nephews will agree to marry the girls if they are educated. Even this reason does not convince the father who concludes by saying that the mother is free to take the burden of educating them. She is the only girl who is sent to graze sheep in her village. If not grazing, she is sent to work in the fields. She is abused as a girl, Dalit and trespasser. On the other hand, her childhood has to face blows from her family that holds her responsible for all that she faces and instructs her to be more careful. She bears all insults and hardships but does not share the same with anyone. She knows that everyone will blame her. It looks as if her father punished her for wanting to go to school by thrusting hard labour on her tender shoulders. Her pertinent questions continue to haunt the researchers, 'Anybody will feel bad if one has to do manual labour always, isn't it?'

In fact, her self-representation shatters the romanticized representations of a young Dalit girl loitering around in an exotic landscape. Her narrative does not allow any romanticization of her labour and her 'rustic beauty'. She is exploited as a girl child in a lower class, lower caste family. She looks at herself as the penalized but her longing for education and her desire to stand on her feet to lead a respectable life boost her confidence to face life.

We come across another young girl, who is full of aspirations about her life. Hers is a very simple and straightforward narration of herself as a young girl who wants to work in order to get educated. She had gone to school and she had also gone to graze cattle in her village. Her experience as a housemaid does not bother her because it gives her access to education. Her focus is on her education. Her goal is to get education. That is her determination. Her child labour became the motivation for her education. Her confidence to shoulder responsibilities in order to access education marks her childhood. Migration, in her case is a source of inspiration.

All the same, though she speaks with confidence and desire for her education, we get a picture of a lower class, lower caste girl anxiously arguing for her basic right and being ready to spend her time and energy to make it come true. For her, education has to be earned and she is ready to earn it. It is not a right nor a privilege like it is in the case of other children. She is not talking about professions for women or a room of one's own but pleading for an opportunity to gain education that should otherwise be her right. Her caste is not what plays a crucial role, according to her. But, it is her class and gender identity that she focuses on.

The same longing for education and hope that education is emancipation expressed by most Dalits is echoed in one of the narratives when the speaker explains her children's education and the problems that they face. She seems to create two worlds—one pervaded by gloom; the other full of hope. And she belongs to the first world, looking towards the other world as a world where discrimination is remarkably less. Education for her is a means of development and progress. She acknowledges that there is some change though not complete change. According to her, this change is also due to their access to education. Moreover, she emphasizes that they have put their children in an English medium school so that their future will be good. She visualizes her children's future. She tries to provide her children what she herself has lost as a child. She is a Dalit woman who has realized the importance of education not for herself but for her future generations. Similarly, the young domestic help also declares proudly that she learnt English when she was in the city and expresses hope that she will be able to study in future.

The MPTC member also repeatedly says that they are not educated. She is able to identify that her lack of education is also one reason for her getting caught in the web of debts as a people's representative. She questions, 'We are working people. How can we study? We have work. I have two sons, one is in college and the other one is studying.' Her lack of education is juxtaposed with the detail that her children are getting educated.

The schoolteacher who has accessed education and is making it accessible to many children says that education and job have earned her a respectable status in society. She now gives her model to her students in order to help them cross obstacles and reach heights in life. It is in a way a compromise because she knows and expresses that she has not yet secured, let alone a respectable status, even an acceptable position in society. She vacillates between the acceptance of her status in society, her self-esteem and her desire to lead a respectable life in society. Her description of her identity and her reflection over her life raise very important questions about the identity of an educated, employed Dalit woman, which is subtly negotiated and discretely discriminated against.

While she seems to be convincing herself that she is successful and has earned a respectable position in society, her experiences and feelings burst out sometimes as she fails to repress them. Her childhood, in her narrative, is not marked by discrimination. She says that she was not aware of caste differences in her childhood but only came to know after she started working. While the other women's narratives in this book are marked by lack of education and longing for education not only as a means of development but also as an escape from caste discrimination, she says that she was unaware of caste consciousness in her childhood and that she did not have to struggle for education. She also makes contradictory statement about her childhood. On one hand she says that her childhood was spent in the most egalitarian and casteless surroundings and on the other she also refers to her friends' responses to her getting the scholarship as a Dalit student. She says, 'When I was a student, nobody in my friends' circle discriminated against me. Everybody knew. I was allotted books as an SC and I used to get a scholarship. They used to feel jealous and say that you get books but we don't.' She proudly declares that it was her privilege to get the scholarship and books. This assertion is what makes her analyse her status as a teacher in a village school from multiple dimensions.

In the case of the NGO volunteer, we see a Dalit woman who has gone a step ahead. She is in the position of convincing others to get educated and bringing them out of child labour. It is not her caste that is a subject for her now but her concern is elimination of child labour. Hers is the story of a 'successful' Dalit woman who returned to studies and motivated child labourers back to school. However, her life could not be set right by herself due to early marriage and loss of opportunities. Hers was almost a child marriage. But, she stood her ground by refusing to go to her husband's house and by continuing her education. Her life became an example for her sisters who achieved higher education. But, 'I am the only one left. Sometimes I feel that everybody is working. I should have waited for some more years to get married. Unnecessarily my parents married me off. I fought with my parents. When I see others I feel that I am telling others but I couldn't set my life right.'

Both the schoolteacher and the NGO volunteer are supposed to educate children, bring them onto the path of success and change. Both of them look at themselves as role models as women who have crossed the obstacles successfully and reached the destinations. But, still they have their own complaints and problems that are not always expressed. However, they acknowledge the fact that it is their education that functions as their savior. It is because of this emancipating capacity of education that education has become an important concern for Dalit women, apart from the issue of survival. It could be a longing to get educated, despair for not being educated or determination for education. Education, for most Dalit women whose oral narratives are recorded here, is the path to development, emancipation and self-reliance.

Most of the written texts in Dalit literature also concentrate on the debates around education and represent the ambition for education among Dalits. Jajula Gowri is one of these writers whose life stands the best example for the hurdles that a woman from a disadvantaged section has to face in order to get education. What the NGO volunteer says in her narrative about her marriage in childhood comes alive here as well. Jajula Gowri was in class eight when her education was stopped and she was married off. The introduction to her book *Mannubuvva* says she took a graduate degree in Distance mode, did her postgraduate degree in Journalism and is into a law course. Neither her introduction nor her autobiographical fiction ends on a negative note though they depict the gloomiest situations and dreadful lives of the downtrodden. Except for a few, Gowri's writings hint at a better tomorrow. Her life is her example to show how one can cross all the obstacles and reach the goal.

Similarly, Jajula Gowri's longing for education, her efforts to come up in life and literary life and her association with the Dalit movement (Madiga literary activities) all mirror her view of herself that she wants to convey to readers. She repeatedly talks about the people who influenced her and inspired her in her journey and these people appear in her stories as well thus representing her models in order to inspire the readers. She says that out of the 25 stories in this collection, 20 stories are based on her background and experiences. The remaining are the stories written on the basis of the incidents that she has clearly seen. She says, 'In all these stories my aim is everybody's welfare. I have imbibed the logic that my mother taught me and goodness that my father has given me as legacy in my stories.'[2]

Bama's autobiography *Karukku*[3] unveils an experience that goes desperately in search of complete emancipation from discrimination. Probably education first and Christianity next, she thinks, will rescue her from ill-treatment. Her hopes are proven wrong and she learns that her status has not changed much even after getting into a nunnery. She realizes that caste differences follow her even into a space that she visualizes as the most egalitarian. This gives rise to her questions such as—Will education really bring in change in the social stratification of the Indian society? What kind of an education will contribute to the elimination of caste hegemony? How did her education and her aspirations help her in defeating the discrimination that she and her people are subjected to?

Similarly, Kumud Pawde[4] also presents a situation where education does not give her complete liberation. As a Dalit woman, she is twice barred from accessing Sanskrit as a language and the 'knowledge' that is available in Sanskrit. She fights her way through humiliations and discouragements at every level. Despite all the hurdles she was able to complete her education and get a postgraduate degree in Sanskrit. But, the purpose of her education was not only to subvert the hegemony of Sanskrit, to prove herself and to acquire knowledge but also to get employment and move up the ladder of social stratification. Her hard-earned degree does not give her any hope as the doubts about her capability in Sanskrit as a Dalit woman haunt her into the recruitment process as well. Disgusted with this, she goes on to do postgraduation in English with the hope that this degree will get her a job. Finally, it is not her Sanskrit degree or the English degree that gets her a job, but it is her changed surname after her marriage to a backward caste man that gets her a job. She discusses this in her autobiography to question the rigid caste boundaries that are invincible even to the tools of education in the case of Dalit communities. One has to remember that these are stories of 'successful' women, who have risen above their people and have become role models to their people. What about people who remain in the same situation and look at education as a savior! Ironically, the role models narrate hardships while others look forward to choose their models.

NOTES

1. Gogu Shyamala, Interview.
2. Jajula Gowri, *Mannubuvva,* n.p.
3. Bama, *Karukku,* tr. Lakshmi Holmstrom, Chennai: Macmillan, 2000.
4. Kumud Pawde, 'The Story of My Sanskrit', in *Poisoned Bread: Translations from Modern Marathi Dalit Literature,* ed. Arjun Dangle, New Delhi: Orient Longman, 1992.

8

Political Power

D R. B.R. AMBEDKAR gave a call to Dalits to achieve political power and he fought with all his strength to create space for Dalits in the arena of political power. His demand for separate electorates finally ended up in tenure-based reservations for the depressed classes. While these reservations are really creating place for Dalits in the political field, quite often Dalits, especially Dalit women are remaining tokens in the political games tossed by the parties and other forces. Dalit women struggle and fight to resist the oppressive structures and to protect their autonomy. We will discuss some such politicians among Dalit women through their narratives and also Ms. Sadalakshmi's biography documented by Gogu Shyamala.

These narratives reveal how these women discuss, identify, and defend the governmental terminology to describe them-selves and their associations. One woman identifies herself as an SC without any hesitation. Some others also refer to some agencies and forces that motivated them and equipped them with the necessary tools. For instance, one woman says that she is not educated but she can write her name. She learnt to write her name when she was in DWCRA (Development of Women and Children in Rural Areas). Her association with DWCRA and its impact on her life result in a slight improvement in envisioning the future of her family and her children.

Similarly, the MPTC member, who never wanted to be one, was forced by 'them' to contest the elections. 'They' also convinced her husband to pressurize her. Who are these 'they'—villagers, community or the political party? What is important is not who they are but the way she emphasizes that she was not interested but was forced to. She does not go to meetings and her husband does not allow her to go. She comes up with many reasons for that which make her sound defensive. We perceive a kind of convincing herself and convincing others that she enjoys certain acceptability and status despite which she does not want to and cannot go there due to some other reasons. But, her emphasis on certain additions like 'why won't they allow' clearly indicate the refusal and the rejection that she faces.

Now I am not going even if they call me. If I go there, my work here will be affected. I won't get hundred rupees if I go there. My husband goes. He goes alone. If I go, both of us have to go. He won't trust me to send me alone. There won't be buses on time. There won't be autos on time.

She knows that they made her contest because she was not educated and they thought she did not know anything. She could understand but her husband could not understand this. Her role is confined to silent signatures on the papers prepared by them. Her husband distrusts her and represents her in meetings. They lost their livelihood as daily labourers after she got into the political position. Like her, other women representatives also do not attend meetings. She raises a crucial point about her getting benefitted from her position. It only increases/extends her toil from fields and home to politics. What about her survival? If accommodating a Dalit woman is called her empowerment, one should carefully listen to the questions that she is asking as to how it will facilitate her own liberation. She says, 'They say that people will become better and big. I am not getting anything. I have to work at home and in the fields and again I have to go there. It is not good.'

There is one more MPTC member who is a landless labourer, uneducated who cannot even sign. She could not do any work after winning the election. She was forced to migrate for livelihood. After winning, she was given neither money nor work. She took a debt of Rs. 1 lakh to spend on the programmes in the three villages that she won from. She had to repay the debt by selling her property, including her marital sacred thread. 'I would have lived as a labourer and fed my children. We would have lived under some tree. Because I am uneducated, they pushed me into this.' It is the same story like the previous one. The so-called political power made them more vulnerable.

She attends meetings but she is not allowed to speak. The previous MPTC member at least says that she was allowed to speak but she did not choose to speak. But, this MPTC member frankly confesses that she was not allowed to speak. Even when there is work, she is not informed. Her signatures are taken, though she lives in extreme poverty with no food to eat and no proper clothes to wear. She spent money on her elections and ran up huge debts to get the government work done for the village. Interest on the loans also add to her penury. She repeatedly says that the village thought that she looked like an innocent woman and so she will win if she contests. She chooses a positive word like 'innocent' but the previous woman boldly said that she was chosen because she could not even sign. This woman, apart from stating that the villagers think well of her, emphatically declares that 'I can't lie, I can't cheat'.

This comes out much more specifically and forcefully in Sadalakshmi's life story. Dalits across the country fought extensively for human rights and political power during 1930s. Poona Pact led to separate electorates for Dalits and tribals—at least partially. Sadalakshmi contested as a reserved candidate in the very first elections in the country in 1952 and was elected to the state assembly. She was the first Madiga woman minister. She carried out responsibilities as a social welfare minister, endowment minister and deputy speaker. Major political leaders like Neelam Sanjeeva Reddy, Damodaram Sanjeevaiah, Kasu Brahmananda Reddy, P.V. Narasimha Rao, Chenna Reddy were all her contemporaries.

She was an active politician (Madiga Dandora, Jai Telangana) and held many positions in the government. She has not published anything but her speeches were distributed as pamphlets. Sadalakshmi being a successful and active politician and activist, was a woman who has proved herself in her personal as well political life. She stands like a role model and inspires others to take her as a role model. She emphasizes that her perseverance and hard work have taken her a long way. For her, nothing is impossible and inaccessible. Her caste, gender and class do not come in her way towards success. She repeatedly asserts the greatness of women.

While other Dalit women reveal a kind of empathy with their community and try to speak for themselves and their community, Sadalakshmi speaks as a woman who is part of women and at the same time not like them.[1] She is not unaware of her Dalit woman's identity and the political implications of it. But, she is keen on establishing herself as a victorious woman. While she is pained by the predicament of women, she takes pride on her success as an efficient politician. She refers to her memories and the appreciations that she got. She tries to construct her identity/image in juxtaposition to other women and remarkable men and also builds it on her memories of her career in the past and on the compliments of her colleagues and her team at that time.

She seems to juxtapose herself with remarkable men with whom she had worked together. She reiterates that she is as capable, efficient and hardworking as they are. As a woman, she is no less. She is not talking about her identity as a Dalit or as a Dalit woman. But, she is talking about women in general and about herself in particular. There is an effort to talk about women whose hidden power is not activated but can be activated as it has happened in her case. That way, she proves how she is different from women who have not proved themselves equal to remarkable men. She is one with women, she believes in women's power and blames the society (patriarchy?) for hiding women's power. At the same time, she is different from them, because she has come out of the imprisonment that they are subjected to.

However, there is another side to the coin too. Not all Dalit women politicians are as successful as Sadalakshmi was. They admit fearlessly and express their anger, frustration and helplessness as mere instruments in the system. What is worse is that Dalit women politicians are being victimized by the powerful politicians. A Dalit woman politician who was interviewed for this book has reluctantly stepped into politics. She does not know anything about her role, responsibility, duty and capability. She is not educated. She does not wish to study. She projects herself as an innocent, ignorant, young, reluctant woman politician. At the same time, she knows that she has become a pawn in the hands of the politicians and that they have chosen her because she is an uneducated, unaware woman, who cannot function without her husband's help. In spite of her knowledge that she is being 'used', she allows them to play with her and misuse her political power. Her consciousness of being a woman dominates that of a politician. She does not say whether she is troubled by her husband's suspicion or not, but, reiterates that she is suspected by her husband and he does not allow her to travel alone. Probably this is one way of her accepting her powerlessness and also convincing herself about his possessiveness as concern for her. She is mediated and manipulated by other politicians while she is represented by her husband who, according to her, is equally ignorant. Where is her space to articulate and be on her own, then?

More than her husband's suspicion it seems her having to attend to too many duties troubles her more. Her statement about having to work at home and in fields and then act as an MPTC member and attend meetings holds a mirror to the women who are expected to play too many roles, perform too many duties, but still remain dependent and deprived of the decision-making power. It is also interesting to see how she constructs her identity as an innocent, helpless, uneducated, victimized, poor, Mala sarpanch. All these identities equally subjugate her and exploit her.

She is not representing her gender problems and caste problems but her economic problems which are the result of the above two and pleads for her livelihood and for release from the burden of debts. Ironically, her office has a scheme to stop migration of labourers in the days of famine and provide food and work to them. But, the sarpanch herself had migrated for work. She lost her work and her political position does not help in her survival. On the other hand, she is buried deep in the abyss of debts. She is the best example of Dalit women in Indian politics. Seats are reserved for Dalit women. But, very cleverly the political parties choose Dalit women who can be pawns in their hands. She repeats that she is innocent and the village also thinks that she is innocent. She is in such a situation that she does not even know that talking about her not making money amounts to corruption and may put her behind the bars and snatch her position away.

The Dalit women present themselves as completely ignorant people as well as very actively involved people politically. One of them leads a very 'ordinary' life, presents a very 'ordinary' narrative. She has no ideologies, no association with any movements and she knows no politics. She does not even use the word 'Dalit' which is the political self-description of the lower castes. Very comfortably she uses the term SCs, that is state-defined, constitution-described identity, which is being countered by Dalits. She emerges as a person belonging to the section that is categorized by the Constitution (Constitutional category). Although she fits into the description that the Constitution has created and hence suggests that she is aware of the Constitutional provisions, she does not express any awareness of Dalit movement or issues that are taken up and debated by Dalits.

On the other hand, there are Dalit women who become conscious about their political identities and fight a political battle. For instance, specific identity of a Madiga emerges in Jajula Gowri's poem 'As I am'. It is written as part of the Madiga agitation for categorization of SC reservations. The writer wants to make her political position clear by describing her identity as well as the political context and her leanings.[2] She lists out how brahmins, kshatriyas and shudras have pushed Dalits to the outskirts and thrust menial jobs on them at the same time branding them as untouchables. Added to that, the hierarchy among Dalits pushes Madigas to the fringes subjecting them to the domination of more successful Malas. Hence, Madigas are on the last step of stratification, kicked by everybody above. To conclude this chapter in Jajula Gowri's words about the internal conflict:

...my own Panchama brother
says that he won't the remaining bones also to survive
grinding me to fine flour
has been haunting me for long with the unity mantra.[3]

NOTES

1. Gogu Shyamala, *Nene Balaanni: Sadalakshmi Batuku Katha*, Hyderabad: Hyderabad Book Trust, 2011.
2. Jajula Gowri, 'As I Am', in *Flowering from the Soil: Dalit Women's Writing from Telugu*, p. 202.
3. Ibid.

9

Family, Companionship, and Sexuality

T HE PREVIOUS CHAPTERS have discussed how the interviewed Dalit women located themselves in their family and community. Either they are talking about their parents and relatives or about their life partners and children. At least three generations of people come into discussion when the women speak. Some stereotypes of life partners are reiterated while some are questioned and some others are dismissed. However, there is a constant engagement with the questions around family, relationships, bonding, responsibilities and roles.

Similarly, there is preoccupation with the companion or companionship in almost all the narratives. They construct partners who are protective, supportive and trusting or the ones who are suspicious and oppressive. Like the presence of men in their life becomes an issue, their absence also becomes an equally important issue. Companionship here is not confined to one dimension of it, but extends to societal, emotional, physical, financial and reproductive issues as well. Their observations about presence and absence of companions construct their idea of family and the changing picture of family in their lives.

Closely connected to these two is the question of sexuality. Not all these women deal with it openly and frankly except the woman who began to live with another man after her husband's death and who said that she had a child with that man. Even there, she is presenting it as her desire to have a child but not as her desire to have a physical relationship with him. There are subtle hints towards their desire and need for companionship when they repeatedly refer to the image of their sexuality in the society. Although none of the interviewed women have chosen to concentrate on their sexuality, it turns out to be very crucial for the discussion of their identity as Dalit women, not only for social and personal reasons but also for religious and cultural reasons.

The MPTC member's husband who was convinced by the village to convince his wife to contest the elections is narrated as a caring husband who works on behalf of his wife. He goes to her office in her place. She does not forget to say that he goes alone. Because, she is not supposed to go alone even if it is her work while he is allowed and also supposed to go as he is helping his wife. She clearly says that he won't trust her to send her alone. But, immediately her statement about his not trusting her is attributed to a convincing reason in the very next line that she spoke—the few buses that are there ply at odd hours.

The families that are narrated by the Chindu women give rise to stimulating discussions. They are deeply rooted in tradition. They accept the caste hierarchy which places them on the last step. The 'homeless', dependent, performing women seem to be redefining the concepts of family, companionship and sexuality. One Chindu woman whose husband expired a few years ago repeatedly talks about the times when he was alive. His absence makes her think about the good times that she had when he was alive. Both of them could earn, perform together;

additionally, no one misbehaved with her. He was a source of support, livelihood and dignity. His absence deprived her of all these things in society.

We see a strong sense of desire for a male companion. She says, 'Won't life be good when husband is there! Even if I am under the tree, my husband will feed me. I will be content. If he were there, we would have earned and settled well.' This is not just emotional, aesthetic and physical relationship but economic companionship as well which is instrumental in the life of a woman artiste who has to live on begging. Her husband passed away and her children went in search of livelihood. In her old age, as a lone Chindu woman who has neither energy nor a companion to perform; neither land nor any stipulated income, she survives on begging in the village. From an artiste, she became a beggar in the absence of her family. For her, family is where the support can come for a woman like her.

This support, as said earlier is not in terms of material survival. But, this is the support that extends to the status of a lower caste/class, performing woman in society. She says that nobody misbehaved with her when her husband was alive. But, she quickly corrects herself by saying that even now no one says anything. But, what she has not said can be clearly heard in what she said—that people misbehaved with her after the death of her husband. Her notion of women's dignity and respectability depends on the shield called 'husband'.

Another Chindu woman also makes the same point about male companions. According to her, 'Man means a shade on the head. With the support of that shade, we used to go into the village and play Yellamma till morning. Wife would play *thalam* while husband acted. We made the man play, we played *thalam*.' She too celebrates the past when her husband was alive. The absence of her husband in her life is generalized by her when she speaks generally about the importance of men in any family. This wish is not only for companionship but also for a husband,

FAMILY, COMPANIONSHIP, AND SEXUALITY

home and people. Like education, husband seems to be the only solution for all her problems.

Both these women refer to the other family members as well. The first woman says that her sons and daughters are not with her. But, she does refer to one daughter. According to her, she has gone in search of livelihood. Apart from that, there are no other details like where she has gone and how she is earning her livelihood. She says that like her and her husband, her daughter is also uneducated. Her daughter is not willing to play *bhagotham*—her traditional art form because she does not like it. Here is a woman who departs from her tradition, hierarchy and restrictions and goes in search of new destinations and lifestyles. While the other Dalit women juxtapose themselves and their children and say that times are better now and that their children are able to access what they were deprived of, this Chindu woman juxtaposes herself and her daughter in terms of their choice of traditions and occupations.

Although the Chindu woman narrates her life and constructs her identity without any awareness of political ideologies and any reference to larger issues, she raises basic questions about caste hierarchy, gender relations, folk art forms and poverty. She speaks as a lone woman battling against the oddities of life and the world. She seems to be talking about herself in the past as a young woman with a companion and in the present as an old woman with no companion to accompany her. She has fond, cherishing memories of the past when their art forms were thriving and when their livelihood was not threatened. Their identity also changes based on the situation they are in. In a few words she puts a powerful depiction of the pathetic condition of the folk art forms. If they play *thaalam* or Chindu, they are only rewarded with hunger. But, if they go for begging, they will at least get food. All the concepts of self-respect and self-reliance go mute here. No movements, no agitations and no measures reach here. It is only a lonely battle of life, which the woman has to fight even if she is tired and lacks physical strength, for she has to survive. The important questions that her narrative raises about the art forms shake the foundations of a society's stock responses to art forms. Art form does not fetch them any money but begging does, ironically.

The other Chindu woman laments that their men are gone and that there is no one to feed her now even if she is starving. Man enjoys a very strong position in this family as a breadwinner but not as the only breadwinner. Man and woman were together in earning to run the family. Absence of any one of them will greatly affect the survival of that family, although man's absence affects the honour and protection of the woman as well. She narrated very important details about her family that—'We were three women in the family. We were co-sisters. Now, we have become hollow. Without husbands, we are destroyed. How do we live? If we have some money, we will drink. Whatever we do, it is for this stomach, they say. Our husbands got AIDS and died.'

Also, her reference to her daughter who has left her mother in search of livelihood throws light on her own identity in juxtaposition. She says that her daughter did not want to be a Chindu performer. The fact, as it is revealed later, is that her daughter was made a *jogini* by her own father. He died of AIDS later. All this shows how women are threatened by other communities and society and also by their own men and traditions as a result of the hegemonic cultures which dominate lower caste life and culture by dictating them and patronizing them. We can perceive the emergence of families with women as heads. Moreover, this emergence provides a novel combination of women who formed a family—co-sisters. Ironically, she broods over those husbands who died of AIDS. They are destroyed because their husbands are dead, according to her. If they were alive, they would have been worse and probably these women's lives would also have been destroyed. Her narrative reflects the transforming families, women's lives and the question of survival.

Her questions and statements about her spouse emphasize the strong familial ties and preservation of institutions like family and marriage that Dalit women look forward to. At the same time, she is also self-contradictory when she says that both she and her husband used to work for their livelihood and again, her husband would have looked after her if he were alive.

Two performing women, one traditional art form and the other revolutionary art form come to our mind at this point. They are Chindu Yellamma and Chandrasri respectively. Chindu Yellamma was a renowned Chindu player of *bhagotham*. She won several awards and honours including the Hamsa award for extraordinary services in art and cultural fields in 1998. Her life narrative[1] brings in very crucial issues for discussion about caste, gender, stratification and art forms. Her story not only records the evolution of her life but also the changing history of the region that she comes from, that is Nizamabad district of Telangana region.

Her life was full of challenges and struggles. But, she also bagged many successes as she made her occupation into her career. In her 82 years of life, she witnessed turning points that probably no other Chindu performing woman had witnessed. There is a marked difference between her life and the life of the Chindu women recorded for this project. However, her story matches with the other Dalit women's stories as to how she was made into a *jogini*. She was a child of four when her father lost his eyesight. The community through rituals 'found' that Yellamma goddess wanted the child to be in her name. Her father resolved to give her for *jogu*. He got the sight and she became Yellamma.

This reminds us of the childhood stories of the Dalit women when they were made into *joginis* without their consent. Yellamma also makes very pertinent observations about the divisions and restrictions of caste and gender. She says that there was no government school in her village in her childhood but there was one Christian school for Malas. Malas and Madigas had separate schools and they strictly adhered to this boundary line. We can see how she is bringing in the question of religion and conversion as she is referring to her childhood and education. She makes it a point to say that none of her people converted into Christianity and that theirs was the 'Aryan' religion. There were no intermarriages and in case there were, the girl would inherit the in-laws' religion.

While she is on the subject of performing women and public space, she says, 'There was no restriction on women playing *bhagotham* . . . we are begging people. We can live if only both man and woman work. If someone says women should not play *bhagotham*, we will ask them to show us some other work. What source do we have except this?'[2] These words echo the words of Chindu women whose narratives are being analysed in this book. It is a working class spirit where man and woman share the work and work together in order to earn a livelihood. Husband's presence is crucial for a woman for not just emotional and physical companionship but also majorly for companionship in struggles of survival. In her words, 'Having a husband is like constructing a house with walls for women'. Here, like it is in the case of the Chindu and *jogini* women whose narratives we have already discussed, husband is a source of protection for women. One can understand this anxiety as emerging from the insecure status of a woman who is given to the temple and in turn to the village. She is not entitled to any rights on her body and on her family.

On the other hand, Yellamma defines companionship also based on the conjugality. She says that she was most of the time away from home as she was busy with performances. Her husband needed someone, obviously a woman, to look after him, cook for him and also fulfil his physical needs. She thought carefully and got her younger sister to marry her husband. Thus, all the three of them lived together. This decision introduces an interesting dimension into her understanding of the marital relationship. She did not hesitate to bring in her sister between him and herself in order to protect their social relationship. It seems as if she wanted to safeguard the family at any cost. She gives a new definition to the family by extending the number of wives.

This also brings up the question of sexuality. Sexuality of her husband and her younger sister are presented very clearly. But, there seems to be an attempt to present herself as an asexual being. She says there was a sister-brother relationship between her and her husband. Similarly, she was approached by many men, as it is said in her biography. Some even tried to threaten and use force. But, she did not succumb to fear or temptation. She stood her ground very firm to prove that she was a performer but not a woman sexually available to men. Is this asexual portrayal a tool of subversion and resistance to the mainstream representation and expectation of performing women, especially the lower caste women?

Another performing woman whose life poses major questions about family, companionship and sexuality is Chandrasri.[3] Chandrasri was a singer, dancer, script writer, director, music composer and led teams of people. She established a Dalit woman's theatre. Taking to performance was in itself a major step in her life. Establishing a Dalit women's theatre was an even more challenging task for her. Chandrasri could cross the barriers laid out for performing women especially from lower castes. She brought the song, dance and performance that were part of Dalit life into the open and presented them from a Dalit woman's perspective.

Her biography is constructed on the basis of the narratives of people who knew Chandrasri and who followed her work carefully. She could transgress the boundaries of caste. She actively participated in Dalit and radical movements. However, her inter-caste marriage led to domestic violence and harassment. That domestic shock eventually led to her early death. Her life raises questions about the serious conflicts involved in the inter-caste marriages especially when one of the couple is a Dalit. Dr B.R. Ambedkar believed that inter-caste marriages are the only means to eradicate caste system in society. But, most Dalit writers have been representing the problematics of such marriages. The companion that she had chosen from a radical movement background became a big hurdle for her association with performance and other movements. Her sexuality also became debatable as her partner constantly harassed her with suspicion about her relationships.

Longing for companionship and family can be seen in the narrative of the *jogini* woman. She says, 'Others have four hands. They will somehow live toiling hard. What about us? We have only two hands.... If somebody says something, their husbands will go to their house to quarrel. But, who will go about us?' Not only that they do not have families but also, as she says, both her people as well as upper caste people also say things about her. So, she distanced herself from everyone like she is distanced by everyone. She comes from a family that succumbed to the pressures of the tradition and surrendered its daughter to the *jogini* tradition but moved away from the societal traditions to educate her brother because he is a boy.

It is intriguing that she does not refer to men in her life and the profession that she is pushed into as a *jogini*. She says that she faces insult in the society as a woman who is available to society, 'When I go out, some fellow says something. My head touches the dust. What should I tell these people, I think. They call me *bogamma*.'[4] The questions about her sexuality also do not appear anywhere in her narrative. However, she poses pertinent questions to the state that banned *jogini* tradition but did not provide alternative sources of livelihood—should she starve to death or become a sex worker?

While she questions how will she could have children without a husband, which could also mean to say that she had no relationships, the other woman who says that she was with a man as she wanted children presents another dimension of women's body, desire, sexuality and reproductive rights. She expresses, like the Chindu women, a similar wish for a male companion. A *jogini* woman also more or less expresses the same concerns and desires. She boldly confesses that her son was born of her lover and not of her husband.

My sin is that this gentleman loved me from the time when my husband was alive. My son was born after going around with him. He is born to him.... After this man touched me, when he said that 'children are born to my wife only after going around with me', I went around with him. I went around for 20–25 years.

She repeatedly says that she was given to an older man who, though sick, was rich. She was never interested in him. She expresses her desire for the other man. But, she also tries to validate her statement by saying that she moved close to him only after making sure that she can have children with him. She continues by saying that she does not even know whether she had a physical relationship with her husband. All that she knows is that she wanted a child. Like the Chindu women speaking about women-centred families, she too speaks about a family that does not live together in one place but is divided between two families. For her, marriage is not binding. She clearly says that she did not think of marriage. Like she expresses her desire for children, she also defines her concept of marriage/husband when she says, '... it is alright even if my husband is old but he has to feed me, even if he goes for manual labour'. Once again, it reminds us of the companionship that Chindu women talked about. Her narrative becomes very complicated due to the complexity in her life and the changes and shifts in her narrative.

She is accused of being a witch and is beaten up. She does not refuse motherhood. She refuses marriage but it is not merely to protest against the patriarchal society, but because she believes that a husband should be able to look after his family. Again, the question of livelihood comes in. It is survival that becomes crucial here. Equality in responsibilities, Dalit women seem to say, will bring in equality in relationships. She negotiates her sexuality by saying that she wanted children at any cost. She comes to us as a woman whose sexuality is neglected, whose desire for motherhood is ignored and whose longing for companionship is never understood. Very boldly she expresses her desire for motherhood, which is the reason according to her for having a relationship with the other man. She shows no hesitation in discussing her relationship. She stands against her people, family and society. She also throws light on the incidents that we often hear about—atrocities on Dalits, especially Dalit women. There are a number of incidents of punishing, beating, harassing, killing Dalit people, accusing them of witchcraft. Not that all these incidents have similar hidden stories behind them, but, this is one hidden fact behind the atrocities.

Here is a woman who declares her desires and sexuality, refuses marriage and defines a husband. While with mainstream feminism it is the question of relationships in and out of wedlock, this Dalit woman defines marriage and the husband she is looking forward to and another Dalit woman caught in tradition of the *jogini* system questions society as to who would want to be her companion. *Jogini* system is an evil social practice that preys on Dalit women. It is all a question of livelihood, survival. *Joginis* are ready to come out of that profession, but will they find an alternative livelihood? Government which makes laws against it and voluntary organizations which work against it—can they solve the problem by providing livelihood to *joginis*? As it is they are alienated by their family. They have no support system to stand by them. What do they do when even their profession is snatched from them? Chindu people choose begging as an alternative. But, for young *jogini* women, who were earlier available to men, will the village set-up allow them to live with dignity and self-respect?

Gogu Shyamala makes very important observations about the reproductive rights of Dalit women while she is on the subject of Feminist Movement in India and Dalit Feminism,

The question of reproductive rights and democratic space within the family system rather than subjugation of women is the central issue in the Feminist Movement in India. Women should be able to enjoy democratic rights within the family. Discussion on these particular issues was started by dominant-caste Feminists, yet the very reproductive rights, social productive rights always remained part of Dalit and also artisan community women's' life. The position taken by Dalit Feminism is that these particular rights of Dalit women, and families in particular, are controlled by the Hindu dominant caste system. And this is going on in all the villages in India as the Dalit families work under them as labourers, since it is the Dalits who only have all the productive agricultural knowledge. So it is mostly Dalit women for whom the reproductive rights are necessary for their family, community and for social production for entire society rather than for mere Dalit Family.[5]

Similarly, Challapalli Swarooparani talks about the tired hands of her mother.[6] Dalit women writers identify themselves with their mother and speak to her. They not only speak to their mother but argue on behalf of her, whether it is with patriarchy or casteist feminism. Challapalli Swarooparani tells her mother that she may not fit in with the urban feminist circles and also questions the feminists as to when they will talk about women in 'kitchenless' houses. She strikes back at patriarchy as well as caste hierarchy.

She questions the roles allotted to women. She breaks the notions attached to womanly behaviour. Without any hesitation, she exposes the attitudes of Dalit men. Once again, this becomes significant as similar debates are going on all over world in the context of movements and literatures of the marginalized. If a woman raises her voice against her people on gender issues, she is with the feminist camp, away from her people's movement. If a woman is with her people's movements and silent over women's rights, then she is faithful to her people and does not require emancipation from her men but requires only liberation from outside hegemony. Do women have to decide between their community and gender? Is there no way they can talk about women like them without getting considered treacherous either to their community movement or feminist movement?

Vijayabharathi studies the status of women, especially lower caste and class women from a Dalit woman's perspective.[7] Ironically, while Puranas are considered to be fictitious by Dalits apart from many others, Vijayabharathi takes them up for a socio-cultural study. While Dalit writers have used Puranas to expose the dubious double standards of Hindu religion, Vijayabharathi uses them to construct a systematic evolution of women's status based on her identities in the Hindu society. Her concern is not just with the past but also with the present so that the past may not be repeated. What is ironic is that she takes the example of the 'ordeal by fire' that Sita was supposed to have been subjected to, though she is specifically talking about the insults and atrocities inflicted on lower caste women. Here, she may not be talking about her identity in particular. But, her identity emerges as she talks about the historical context of atrocities on Dalit women. She depicts herself as a Dalit woman who expresses her anguish for the age-old cruelty of Hindu society towards Dalit women as well as solidarity for the woman question in general, especially that of lower classes.

Talking about sexuality, 'Dalit Feminist Manifesto' marks a very significant point in Dalit women's writing by expressing its concern for Dalit women's predicament from a feminist perspective. It emphasizes solidarity of Dalit women, women, as well as concerned people towards social change. While the struggle is against the casteist patriarchy, the plea is to the upper caste women, specifically. This establishes the identity of Dalit women and also argues for support from women of other castes. In this context, one important issue regarding identities needs to be mentioned and noted. 'Dalit Feminist Manifesto' is written or rather drafted by the students of an elite university situated in a cosmopolitan atmosphere. They are aware of various ideologies, movements and debates. This establishes a clear distinction between this text and other texts dealt with in this project although the writers of 'Dalit Feminist Manifesto' are arguing for solidarity.

Significantly, the writers come up with the concept of Dalit feminism. Although they do not establish clearly as to what this concept means, it gives a unique identity to Dalit women who want to fight against casteist patriarchy. Apart from calling for solidarity, they explain how these sections— that is upper caste and Dalit women, are both being victimized by casteist patriarchy. While they do not say no overtly to the upper caste feminism, they express the desire to form a common platform for all women. It is in this context that we are reminded of similar debates in different situations. For instance, Jackie Huggins argues how all women cannot be same,[8] Bell Hooks[9] finds fault with the strategic moves to push black woman away from feminism thus keeping them away from their own politics and making them believe that race is more important than gender while both race and gender are equally repressive and oppressive factors on black women. It is interesting to note how while Shulamith Firestone in her book *The Dialectic of Sex*[10] argues that racism is sexism extended, Bell Hooks says that sexism is racism extended. 'Dalit Feminist Manifesto' addressing women of all castes in itself reveals its concern and need for solidarity among women. The two sets of Indian women that are being created by society not only bifurcate women but also equally punish them, though in diverse ways.

NOTES

1. *Nenu Chindu Yellammanu.*
2. *Nenu Chindu Yellammanu*, p. 55.
3. Joopaka Subhadra, ed., *Chandrasri Yaadilo: Rachanala Sankalanam*, Hyderabad: Mattipulu Rachayitrula Vedika, 2013.
4. Devadasis who gradually settled into prostitution were given the caste name *bogam*.
5. Gogu Shyamala, Interview.
6. Challapalli Swarooparani, 'My Mother', in *Flowering from the Soil: Dalit Women's Writing*, pp. 277–81.
7. *Nallapoddu*, pp. 126–8.
8. Jackie Huggins, *Sister Girl: The Writings of Aboriginal Activist and Historian*, St. Lucia: University of Queensland Press, 1998.
9. Bell Hooks, *Ain't I a Woman.*
10. Shulamith Firestone, *The Dialectic of Sex: The Case for Feminist Revolution*, Farrar, Straus and Giroux, 2003.

10

Conclusion Later Developments

THIS PROJECT, AS was mentioned in the earlier chapters, was taken up during 2003–5. Telangana movement was a memory of the past and a wish of the present at that time. Later it intensified and finally the dream of the people was realized in 2014. Many sacrifices and battles went into the making of the new state of Telangana.

Almost six decades of the struggle for a separate Telangana state witnessed several changes in identities, alliances, arguments and leaderships. Especially the past phase of the long movement that started in 2009 brought forth the revisiting of many pasts and revising of several identities. Such developments were also reflected on the caste and subcaste movements, minority movements and women's movements. In a sense, the crucial dimensions of identity politics/movements faced an unsettling jolt which proved to be revelatory for them.

It will be apt to conclude this book on Dalit women's narratives and identities by discussing the developments that happened after this project was completed. It is also important to study these developments in order to understand the region as a site of people's movements during which people of different identities came together, got separated and fought against each other. This chapter discusses the arguments related to caste and gender during the making of Telangana movement from Dalit women's perspective. I base my discussion majorly on the prose writings of the Dalit woman writer Subhadra Joopaka, though I bring in select writings of Gogu Shyamala and Challapalli Swarooparani for passing references and comparisons.

It is true that larger movements bring people together by forcing them, for a while, to set aside their differences and diversities. It is also true that the movements bring together changes in personal relationships and vice versa. Telangana movement witnessed people from varied castes, classes, professions, age groups and regions getting united for a separate state and identifying themselves with the identity of the state of Telangana. However, like the identity of Indians, the identity of Telanganites also had to take the questions about crucial issues such as caste/subcaste and religion.

Dalit movement and Dalit literature have witnessed debates about not only subcaste and gender issues among Dalit communities but also about the issue of the region. Migration to Rangoon and the missionary education by conversion into Christianity in late nineteenth century and early twentieth century gave the Dalit communities a better position in terms of education, land rights, employment and religious freedom in Andhra. Dalit communities in Telangana and Rayalaseema did not have these avenues due to various reasons. These differences led to different standards of progress and development for the Dalit communities. On the other hand, the Telangana movement clearly created a binary of Telangana and Coastal Andhra (which includes Rayalaseema) that went on to stand for oppositional positions of one wanting a separate state and the other wanting to be together as a united state. Caste and religious factors added to these fractured identities. It is against this backdrop that this chapter will discuss how the Dalit women enact their multi-dimensional identities.

Challapalli Swarooparani, in her article, raises crucial questions about the concept of rights and habitations. Referring to the arguments of the people from Andhra that their rights of location/habitation are being curtailed and that all people of Andhra should unite irrespective of their caste, religion and linguistic differences, she hits at them saying that Dalit communities, in whichever region they are, are deprived of their rights, are isolated and marginalized. How can they raise the question of solidarity and unity when they have never extended the same to the Dalit communities? Dalits can understand the argument of people from Telangana for a separate state as they have been deprived of opportunities and marginalized in every respect; their language, culture and lifestyle are also ridiculed. Dalits would rather declare solidarity with Telangana movement, whichever region they belong to.

One cannot forget the emergence of the women writers' forum that started as one and got divided into two. It started in solidarity of all women and was divided into solidarity with women writers of certain identities. Challapalli Swarooparani declares that the Democratic Women Writers' Forum was established for solidarity among like-minded women writers of different sections. If we recall the agenda of *Mattipulu*, which includes Dalit, tribal, minority and backward caste women writers of Rayalaseema, Andhra and Telangana, it clearly records the forum's decision to support Telangana movement. It has witnessed the active participation of Dalit women, who are activists, employees, students and those who are associated with NGOs articulating their arguments in different forums.

Joopaka Subhadra in her column 'Maakka Mukkupulla Geenne Poyindi'[1] acknowledges such solidarity when she says,

127

We have been fighting continuously for the past sixty years because those who co-existed with us for the past sixty years saw us as others, established their authority over our lands, jobs, resources, language, history and civilization; they have encroached and oppressed us. Only some Dalit organizations in Seemandhra have stood by Telangana people in these sixty years and fought in support. No Seemandhra upper caste groups have supported Telangana struggles ... hope that the bahujans living in the shade of Hyderabad as Seemandhras will welcome and respect the declaration of Telangana and support the Telangana people and that they will not carry the hegemonic agenda of the Seemandhra upper caste people. Bahujans and bahujan women should be well in Seemandhra and Telangana.

There is an attempt to reinterpret and revisit history not only from the perspective of Telangana but from the perspective of Dalit communities which is also against the Brahmani-cal Hindutva ideology. The Telangana Liberation Day on 17 September 1948 has been highlighted and Police Action has been justified and the event has been portrayed as unification of the state with the nation. Dalit and minority intellectuals have been arguing that it was not Police Action but Military Action and that of the Hindu jagirdars, zamindars and deshmukhs under the Nizam's rule conspired with the nationalist Hindus and contributed to this treachery. Subhadra argues that this is the best example for the distortion of the story and that this is typical Hindu autocracy. She continues to say that this invasion called the Military Action was the result of the upper caste zamindars, jagirdars, deshmukhs, patels and patwaris working under the Hyderabad state ruler as a Muslim. What happened in the name of the National Movement was the Hindu movement. This Hindu weapon eliminated Ambedkar's communal award for Dalits through Gandhi. It is due to Gandhi's Hindu argument that Poona Pact was brought to enslave the Dalits once again. She draws the attention of the readers to the fact that most of the people who were targeted and massacred during these incidents

128

in Telangana were Muslims. She says that this Military Action attacked the state on all four sides, massacred millions of people and conquered the Telangana state without facing any counter-attack. Such a military attack and invasion deprived all special protection and rights for the local people. This is an interesting way of connecting the past, present and future of Telangana.[2]

Subhadra intensifies the questions against patriarchy in the context of rebuilding of Telangana. Either there are upper caste men or at the most a couple of upper caste women in any meeting on rebuilding of the new state. She sarcastically says that there won't be space in mobile phone messages as well as the stage when it comes to women. Even if there is space, there won't be time to give them the mike. According to her, there is no space in phones and on stage as well as in their minds. She comes down heavily on the Telangana movement that did not take the representation of women as a serious issue. While she is discussing how dangerous it is for the women when no forces take this issue seriously, she quotes an anecdote to emphasize her point,

One Bahujan association leader invited me for a round table on women's empowerment in the reconstruction of Telangana. As I was unhappy with the way meetings were pushing aside women, I went to see the bahujan castes women's groups to speak. Male leaders were sitting at the main tables in the round table. The leader who organized the meeting was presiding. On both sides of the room at the tables were sitting women from the bahujan castes.

She expresses her anger about Telangana movement not being able to construct the histories of women who fought for Telangana. Acknowledging the contribution of Yadava Rani, Sadalakshmi, Eswaribai, and Zeenat Sajida, Subhadra asserts that Telangana has to be newly constructed but not reconstructed and that the caste and gender discrimination should disappear in the neo-construction (3 February 2014).

Subhadra discusses in detail about the powerlessness of lower castes and women in the Telangana region due to various reasons. She comes up on behalf of *Matti Mahila Sangham* with a list of demands. This functions as a continuation of the resolution of *Mattiupulu*. This also draws the outline/blueprint for the bahujan Telangana which is not just a geographical entity but a new state of social justice built on the dismantled foundations of feudal systems. Following are the demands of the women of the soil that should be implemented in Telangana:

Residential hostels should be established in every *mandal* for the women of the soil.

3 acres of land should be given to these women.

Every political party should reserve at least 30 per cent of its seats for the women of the soil.

Reservations for these women should be declared in private firms.

Industries that can increase the employment opportunities for agricultural labourer women should be established.

Loans should be sanctioned on priority for women of occupational castes.

Women should be given loans in women's corporations on caste basis.

It should be arranged to sanction 50 per cent of loans in BC, SC and ST corporations to women.

These women should be provided employment from the village level.

Creches should be established in villages.

Leadership and empowerment of women of the soil should be increased to 50 per cent in political constructions.

The next chief minister of Telangana should be a woman of the soil.

Women's police stations should be established in every *mandal* for the safety of women.

Recommendations of Justice Punnaiah Commission on elimination of caste system should be sincerely implemented.

This agenda extends from representation for women to political leadership. This is part of conceptualization and visualization of a new state from a Dalit woman's perspective which is trying to construct a solidarity network of people, especially women who have lost all agency and who are struggling to resist the casteist and patriarchal forces colonizing their minds, bodies and lives.[3]

She comments on the absence of women in the committees constituted for the reconstruction of Telangana and wonders if it is not social justice to talk on behalf of women and about women's participation. She also emphasizes that it is a pity that women's voices, those of downtrodden as well as the upper caste, seem to believe that talking about gender equality will be against Telangana and that Telangana issue will be side-tracked if anything else other than the separate state is discussed as part of the agenda.[4]

Similarly, Subhadra invokes Dr B.R. Ambedkar who questioned why the upper castes did not take up scavenging if it is as sacred as it was preached for the Dalit communities. The subcastes and their professions also become crucial here.[5] She strongly condemns the politics of accommodating women in the wings and points out how women of all sections are treated during the employee association elections, despite which women stood together and gave a tough fight. The threats included collapsing of families, labelling as firebrands, tearing of pamphlets and banners, putting condoms in women's toilets and writing obscenities in lifts.

Bathukamma festival is debated from various dimensions and different belief systems. While some think it is Hindu in nature and association, some others argued that it is secular and is played by women of all castes, classes and religions. While some said that it is a festival meant for privileged sections, some others believed that this festival was always open for women of all castes and classes. Some voices showed historical evidences while some others struck them off as mere fluid oral narratives without any base.

Bathukamma festival is situated in rural, working class, Telangana culture that represents a close association with nature. Unlike many ritualistic Hindu festivals, Bathukamma festival turns heaps of flowers into a deity. Telangana state which came into existence in 2014 after six decades of movements for a separate state chose it for official celebration as it played an instrumental role in bringing people together and establishing a cultural icon during the movement. This festival chooses the public sphere as its site and hence, as a women's festival, brings women out of their homes and gives them a common space for sharing, playing and singing.

However, there are questions surrounding such a festival especially when it is chosen to become the cultural symbol for a state. Although the festival is projected as a secular festival open to all religions and castes, the Hindu traits of it and the upper caste appropriation and lower caste exclusions from it cannot be ruled out. It might be a good strategy for the women and especially Dalit women to reclaim that space and demolish the restrictions of exclusion. But, unfortunately, this can also make them remain part of the governmental strategy to sentimentalize people's emotions and traditions towards a women's festival that is celebrated with song and dance.

Subhadra Joopaka, who actively participated in the Telangana movement argues vociferously that women played an instrumental role in history and in Telangana movement. But, they are not to be seen in the decision-making committees and forums in the newly established state. On the other hand, they are given the entire space in the Bathukamma festival. The feminization of the festival and the celebration is also a design of limiting women to a feminine space which does not pose a threat to the space and position occupied by men. Women who participated in the movement are reveling in song and dance while men who were part of the movement are lost in state-making. This is not only about allotment of space but also about assignment of roles and designing of behaviours and choices.

Although Subhadra says that they wanted to celebrate the festival to mark the women's empowerment, it means bringing religion into government space and making women employees sing and dance. Does it also mean that they are not capable of intellectual activity but are only good at and interested in dancing around the heaps of flowers reiterating the stereotype of the association between nature and women?

Even if the celebration of this festival is considered to be a space exclusively for women for their meetings, interactions and celebrations, the state's decision to celebrate it with its money in the office space is nothing but appropriation of people's culture by the government to protect its institutional interests and demean women's localized and situated knowledge and celebratory systems in festival spaces, moods and rituals.

Subhadra points out that women's Bathukamma has become a male festival. It is not a festival meant for men but wholly for women. Yet, men stepped in to conduct the festival, instruct women, obstruct the funds that they have received, occupied the space on the stage. This actually turns men into audience sitting in an elevated position. So, women who fought for the movement and who are entitled to celebrate the movement have all rights to celebrate the festival becoming the site of gaze for men. Bringing women back into the fold of religion and ritual programmes is one way of ensuring that women stick to their stereotypes as this will fetch them state incentives too.

Subhadra criticizes the fact that men appropriated the conduct of the festival when the Telangana government declared it as the state festival and when women wanted it to be celebrated as women's empowerment Bathukamma to resolve women's problems. When the chief minister responded favourably,

TNGO (Telangana Non-Gazetted Officers) associations created hurdles. Suddenly they convened meetings and Bathukamma celebrations and formed committees in districts and cities. Instead of women playing Bathukamma independently, men sat on the stage lecturing and exhibiting their huge cut outs. They enjoyed making the women employees play Bathukamma off the stage, in between men also played, arranged disco songs and DJs. They even insulted the women, flowers and Bathukammas. They made the members of the women's wing of NGO forum in the state secretariat play Bathukamma in competition with the women of independent forum. As the wing women were incited against the independent women, they had to play the flower Bathukamma as the war Bathukamma. The festival on which all women happily sing their stories and histories with flowers and lake waters was transformed into male Bathukammas.

Subhadra questions: 'Do we women exist in Telangana? If we do, where are we and what has happened to us? What is to be done when political, economic, social, cultural and philosophical helplessness surrounds us? What do we do? We are looking like living corpses to ourselves.'[6] This article titled 'Male Rule Without Women' once again excavates the women's history in Telangana and points out that women rulers existed in the so called feudal era but not in the present era of globalization. Women were there in the Telangana movement; fought as cadre in the constructive struggles and were beaten up during non-cooperation, all people's strike, processions, rasta rokos and others. But, they were never recognized as capable of holding leadership. Women do not know that their place is only for number strength. Whether it is meetings with slogans, million marches, holding hands, rail rokos or playing Bathukammas or carrying bonams.

She goes further by saying that 'movements, naxal movements, dalit and dandora movements also did not recognize and respect women's leadership. All these movements did not mention a word about women in their histories'. Same is the case with Telangana. Development is not complete without women's development. Formation of women's protection committee does not mean liberation of women. Where is the political representation for women in the newly formed state of Telangana?

Subhadra says, 'It is not just male and female, there are many other gender differences in society. Upper caste patriarchy was cruel and mean towards transgenders and hijras and resorted to several attacks and atrocities. If the men and women of lower castes have hatred for them, we have to think that it has come from hegemonic patriarchal mindset.'[7] Dalit women's solidarity reaches out to transgender people as they join the transgender people's protests and celebrations. Saying that it is the responsibility of all to protect the human rights of hijras, Subhadra states that

We used to lament that only untouchable women are taken for granted in this society and that they are the most insulted whose needs are not fulfilled and who have no human rights. But the sorrow of the male hijras and trans women is greater than ours. No civil societies are moved even when rowdies and police beat up, attack and kill them. They face humiliation and severe opposition in everyday life. Society looks at hijras as if they are not human beings.[8]

One can perceive how Dalit women's questions are becoming increasingly sharpened in Telangana. Theirs is not only a struggle for self-esteem and their writings are not just an expression of resistance. Their journey is towards political power apart from other forms of empowerment of Dalit women and their liberation from the oppressive hierarchy controlled by men of privileged as well as underprivileged sections and women of privileged sections.

NOTES

1. *Bhumika Strivada Patrika* (Telugu), 3 September 2013, Hyderabad.
2. Ibid., 1 October 2013.
3. Ibid., 2 May 2014.
4. Ibid., 2 August 2014.
5. Ibid., 3 October 2014.
6. Ibid., 1 January 2015.
7. Ibid., 2 December 2014.
8. Ibid., 4 February 2015.

Bibliography

Adams, Howard, *A Tortured People: The Politics of Colonization*, Penticton BC: Theytus Books, 1995.

Allen, Paula Gunn, ed., *Spider Woman's Granddaughters*, New York: Fawcett Columbine, 1989.

Anand, Mulk Raj and Eleanor Zelliot, eds., *An Anthology of Dalit Literature,* New Delhi: Gyan Publishing House, 1992.

Anand, S., *Touchable Tales: Publishing and Reading Dalit Literature*, Pondicherry: Navayana, 2003.

Bagchi, Jasodhara, ed., *Indian Women: Myth and Reality*, Hyderabad: Sangam Books (India) Limited, 1995.

Bassnett, Susan and Harish Trivedi, eds., *Post-colonial Translation: Theory and Practice*, London: Routledge, 1999.

Bathla, Sonia, *Women, Democracy and the Media: Cultural and Political Representations in the Indian Press*, New Delhi: Sage Publications, 1998.

Bharathi, Thummapudi, *A History of Telugu Dalit Literature*, Delhi: Kalpaz Publications, 2008.

Charsley, Simon R. and G.K. Karanth, eds., *Challenging Untouchability: Dalit Initiative and Experience from Karnataka*, New Delhi: Sage Publications, 1998.

Clarke, Sathianathan, *Dalits and Christianity: Subaltern Religion and Liberation Theology in India*, New Delhi: Oxford University Press, 1999.

Dangle, Arjun, ed., *Poisoned Bread: Translations from Modern Marathi Dalit Literature*, Hyderabad: Orient Longman, 1992.

Dharmanna, Kusuma, *Makoddi Nalladorathanam*, Hyderabad: Hyderabad Book Trust, 2003 (1921).

Gaikwad, Laxman, *The Branded*, tr. P.A. Kolhatkar, New Delhi: Sahitya Akademi, 1998.

Ghurye, G.S., *Caste and Race in India*, Bombay: Popular Prakashan, 2004, 1932.

Gupta, Dipankar, *Interrogating Caste: Understanding Hierarchy and Difference in Indian Society*, New Delhi: Penguin Books, 2000.

Hooks, Bell, *Ain't I a Woman: Black Women and Feminism*, Boston MA: South End Press, 1981.

Jaiswal, Suvira, *Caste: Origin, Function and Dimensions of Change*, New Delhi: Manohar, 1998.

Jadhav, Narendra, *Outcaste: A Memoir*, New Delhi: Penguin, 2003.

Jenkins, Richard, *Social Identity*, London: Routledge, 1996.

Joe, Rita, *Poems of Rita Joe*, Halifax: Abanaki, 1978.

Kannabiran, Kalpana, ed., *The Violence of Normal Times: Essays on Women's Lived Realities*, New Delhi: Women Unlimited, 2005.

Kishwar, Madhu, *Off the Beaten Track: Rethinking Gender Justice for Indian Women*, New Delhi: Oxford University Press, 1999.

Kumar, Ashutosh, ed., *Rethinking State Politics in India: Regions within Regions*, New Delhi: Routledge, 2011.

Kumar, Raj, *Dalit Personal Narratives: Reading Caste, Nation and Identity*, New Delhi: Orient BlackSwan, 2010.

Kumar, Ravi, *Venomous Touch: Notes on Caste, Culture and Politics*, tr. Azhagarasan, Kolkata: Samya, 2009.

Kotani, H., ed., *Caste System, Untouchability and the Depressed*, New Delhi: Manohar, 1997.

Kshirsagar, R.K., *Dalit Movement in India and its Leaders*, New Delhi: M.D. Publications Pvt. Ltd., 1994.

Lakshminarasaiah, G., *The Essence of Dalit Poetry: A Socio-Philosophic Study of Telugu Dalit Poetry*, Hyderabad: Dalita Sana Publications, 1999.

Limbale, Sharankumar, *Towards an Aesthetic of Dalit Literature: History, Controversies and Considerations*, tr. Alok Mukherjee, Hyderabad: Orient Longman, 2004.

Mayaram, Shail, *Against History, Against State: Counterperspectives from the Margins*, Delhi: Permanent Black, 2004.

Mendelson, Oliver and Marika Vicziany, *The Untouchables: Subordination, Poverty and the State in Modern India*, New Delhi: Foundation Books, 2000.

Mines, Mattison, *Public Faces, Private Voices: Community and Individuality in India*. Delhi: Oxford University Press, 1996.

Mohanty, Manoranjan, ed., *Class, Caste, Gender*, New Delhi: Sage Publications, 2004.

Moon, Vasant, *Growing Up Untouchable in India*, tr. Gail Omvedt, New Delhi: Sage Publications, 2001.

Nageshbabu, Madduri, *Velivada: Kavita Samputi*, Narasaraopeta: Srija Publicaitons, 1995.

———, ed., *Vidi Akasam: Ambedkarist Prema Kavitvam*, Paloncha: Dalita Sana Publications, 1999.

Nag, Kingshuk, *Battleground of Telangana: Chronicles of an Agitation*, Noida: HarperCollins, 2011.

Nair, Rukmini Bhaya, *Lying on the Postcolonial Couch: The Idea of Indifference*, New Delhi: Oxford University Press, 2002.

———, ed., *Translation, Text and Theory: The Paradigm of India*, New Delhi: Sage Publications, 2002.

Narayan, Badri and A.R. Misra, *Multiple Marginalities: An Anthology of Identified Dalit Writings*, New Delhi: Manohar, 2004.

Omvedt, Gail, *Rethinking Revolution: New Social Movements and the Socialist Tradition in India*, New York: An East Gate Book, 1993.

———, *Ambedkar: Towards an Enlightened India*, New Delhi: Penguin Books, 2004.

Padmarao, Katti, *Pitrusvamyavyavasthalo Stri*, Poonuru: Lokayata Prachuranalu, 2003.

Philip, Kavita, *Civilising Natures: Race, Resources and Modernity in Colonial South India*, Hyderabad: Orient Longman, 2003.

Phule, Jyotirao, *Gulamgiri (Banisatvam)*, tr. Eluri Ramaiah, Hyderabad: Hyderabad Book Trust, 1993.

Poitevin, Guy and Hema Rairkar, *Indian Peasant Women Speak Up*, tr. Michel Leray, Hyderabad: Orient Longman, 1993.

Rajasekhar, Patteti and Nagappagari Sundarraju, eds., *Gundedappu: Dalita Kavita Sankalanam,* Hyderabad: Dalita Sahitya Vedika, 1995.

Ray, Raka, *Fields of Protest: Women's Movements in India*, New Delhi: Kali for Women, 2000.

Reed-Gilbert, Kerry, *The Strength of Us as Women: Black Women Speak*, Charnwood: Ginninderra Press, 2000.

Rege, Sharmila, ed., *Sociology of Gender: The Challenge of Feminist Sociological Knowledge,* New Delhi: Sage Publications, 2003.

Sarkar, Sumit, *Writing Social History*, New Delhi: Oxford University Press, 1997.

Shah, Ghanshyam, ed., *Dalit Identity and Politics,* Cultural Subordination and the Dalit Challenge, vol. 2, New Delhi: Sage Publications, 2001.

Shyamala, Gogu, *Nallapoddu: Dalita Strila Sahityam 1921–2002*, Hyderabad: Hyderabad Book Trust, 2003.

Simon, Sherry, ed., *Culture in Transit: Translation and the Changing Identities of Quebec Literature*, Montreal: Vehicle Press, 1995.

———, *Gender in Translation: Cultural Identity and the Politics of Transmission*, London: Routledge, 1996.

Singharoy, Debal K., ed., *Social Development and the Empowerment of Marginalized Groups*, New Delhi: Sage Publications, 2001.

Sivasagar, 'On-going History', tr. Archana Chowhan, *Indian Literature*, no. 200: November–December 2000, vol. XLIV, no. 6, p. 108, New Delhi: Sahitya Akademi.

Srinivas, M.N., *Collected Essays*, New Delhi: Oxford University Press, 2002.

———, 'Caste in Modern India', in *Class, Caste, Gender: Caste in Indian Politics*, ed. Manoranjan Mohanty, New Delhi: Sage Publications, 2003.

Stri Shakti Sanghatana, *Manaku Teliyani Mana Charitra: Telangana Raithanga Poratamlo Strilu,* Hyderabad: Hyderabad Book Trust, 1986.

Sudhakar, Yendluri, *Darky: Nalladrakshapandiri*, Secunderabad: J.J. Prachuranalu, 2002.

———, *Vargeekaraneeyam: Dalita Deergha Kaavyam,* Rajahmundry: Manasa and Manogna Prachuranalu, 2004.

Swarooparani, Challapali, 'Dalit Women's Writing in Telugu', *Economic and Political Weekly*, vol. 33, issue 17, 25 April 1998, ws 21 to ws 24.

Taneti, James Elisha, *Caste, Gender, and Christianity in Colonial India: Telugu Women in Mission*, New York: Palgrave Macmillan, 2013.

Thapar, Romilla, *Narratives and the Making of History: Two Lectures*, New Delhi: Oxford University Press, 2000.

Thorat, Vimal, 'Dalit Women have been left behind by the Dalit Movement and the Women's Movement', http://www.sabrang.com/cc/archive/2001/may01/cover1.htm.

Valmiki, Omprakash, *Joothan: A Dalit's Life*, tr. Arun Prabha Mukherjee, Kolkata: Samya, 2003.

Viramma, Josiane Racine and Jean-Lue Racine, *Viramma: Life of a Dalit*, New Delhi: Social Science Press, 2000.

Womack, Craig S., *Red on Red: Native American Literary Separatism*, Minneapolis: University of Minnesota Press, 1999.

Zelliot, Eleanor, *From Untouchable to Dalit: Essays on the Ambedkar Movement*, New Delhi: Manohar, 2001 (1992).

———, *Dalits and the Democratic Revolution: Dr Ambedkar and the Dalit Movement in Colonial India,* New Delhi: Sage Publications, 1994.

Index

www.ingramcontent.com/pod-product-compliance
Lightning Source LLC
Chambersburg PA
CBHW031537260326
41914CB00032B/1854/J